CLEAN DOORSTEPS
TALKS TO WOMEN'S MEETINGS

CLEAN DOORSTEPS

TALKS TO WOMEN'S MEETINGS

BY

WILLIAM J. MAY

AUTHOR OF

Sisterhood Prayers and Devotions
According to Mary-Martha
The Opinions of Mary-Martha
Muddled Arithmetic
&c., &c.

LONDON
THE EPWORTH PRESS
(EDGAR C. BARTON)
25-35 CITY ROAD, E.C.1

First Edition, 1935

Made and Printed in Great Britain by H. E. Warne Ltd., St. Austell

CONTENTS

INTRODUCTION

ONLY THE WOMEN'S MEETING

THE Women's Meeting has never been regarded as a gathering of great importance. It is almost the only regular gathering of the Church concerning which we are not asked for an Annual Schedule. That fact alone is a measure of its unimportance. No Conference has ever appointed a Commission to inquire into its efficiency. People knew that a cup of tea was a part of its programme, almost a ritual, and that the members had an annual trip at their own expense, but, beyond that, few people took much interest in it. It was only the Women's Meeting.

But of late years the Women's Meeting has been coming into its own. Preachers have begun to recognise that thirty or fifty women on Monday afternoon may be as well worth preparing for as a handful of well-established saints at Tuesday evening's preaching service. And sometimes as we have looked into their faces, and have gone into their homes, there has been an appeal for our best, almost a demand for it, inspired by a deep need, which no one could ignore or deny. We have felt that they were seeking something more than a cup of strong tea and Sankey's hymns.

For so many of them the Women's Meeting is the only break in the week. The claims of home and children make it impossible for them to come to Church on Sundays unless Jim is willing to stay at home to mind the children, and usually he is not. Yet the demand of the life of every day upon their patience and courage ; their faith and hope, is unceasing. The Women's Meeting is an opportunity not only for a rest and the privilege of a cup of tea which they have not had to make for themselves, but to hear some message of faith and hope ; to have some fellowship with the spiritual and the Eternal which shall renew their strength ; to give them something to think about more inspiring than doorstep gossip. The women for whom these talks were first prepared were the real inspiration of them. I could never have prepared them apart from my fellowship with working women in many parts of England and a sympathy with their needs.

These talks have kept close to the common things of everyday for many reasons. Doorsteps and mending baskets ; shop windows and the postman's knock, were the things in which they were interested.

Women who had done a heavy day's washing before they come to the Meeting were too tired to listen to sermons ; they needed to be entertained as well as taught, and I tried to exercise the ministry of laughter as well as the ministry of preaching. Yet I always endeavoured to keep the end in view, and as a woman said to me one afternoon : ' You start from some strange places but you always come back to the Bible in the end.'

They were concerned with everyday topics for this reason also ; that they are topics which are unforgettable. Talk to a woman about mending socks or making dresses, and the next time she is engaged on those tasks something of your message will come back to her and the lesson will be re-taught. That was the way of the Master-Teacher, the Lord Jesus. When He talked of patching clothes or making bread, or the hen with her chickens that scratched about the door, each time that men saw them they were reminded of what He had said. That was the purpose of these talks on homely themes and the endeavour was not in vain.

These addresses are published in the hope that they will prove helpful and suggestive to those who have to conduct and address Women's Meetings. They will be found most helpful if they are regarded, not so much as ready-made addresses as suggested topics and as some material which speakers can use as seed-thoughts for the good ground of their own minds so that the addresses shall become enriched with their own thoughts and ideas.

Some of these talks have appeared in the weekly column I contribute to *Joyful News*, under the title of ' Monday Afternoon,' and some in the *Methodist Church Record*. I am deeply grateful to the Editors for the hospitality of their pages and for the privilege of reprinting them.

Oldbury, Birmingham.   WILLIAM J. MAY.
    September, 1935.

CLEAN DOORSTEPS

I

BEGINNING AGAIN

My friend Mrs. Grump says that all this fuss about the first of January is just tomfoolery. After all, what difference does a date on a calendar make? The first of January is not different from any other day. Grates must be cleaned and meals prepared and pots washed, just as if it was the fifth of July or the thirteenth of November, so why make a fuss. That may be perfectly true, but there is something within us which will not agree that it is all the truth. The New Year does mean a new beginning and a fresh start, in spite of all the Mrs. Grump's of this world and just because we know we have been given a fresh start we find ourselves singing—we scarcely know why.

We have turned a fresh page in the Book of Life, and we recapture the feeling we had when we started a new exercise book when we were children at school. There was not much hope of the old one, too many blots and finger prints, too many exercises marked 'wrong.' But there is a thrill in starting a new one. Somehow, new things always affect us in that way, especially if we do not get them very often. Every woman feels a little better if she is wearing a new frock, holds her head higher if she has a new hat, walks a little more proudly if she is wearing new shoes, as long as they are not

pinching too badly. New things really do count fo
something, even new years.

The Same Old You

' But it is the same old you,' my friend Mrs. Grump
insists again. ' You will see the same face in the mirror
It will not be a new face because you try to persuade
yourself it is a new year. There will be the same old
disposition, just as ready to flare up like a fire on which
oil has been thrown ; you will get just as mad if the
chimney smokes or if baby is cross. So what difference
does it make ? ' But there are two sides to all that
If I cannot change my face I can alter my looks. The
face a woman shows the butcher when she is complaining
about Sunday's joint is not the face she shows Jim
when he brings his pay envelope home on Friday
night. A smile instead of a frown does more to im
prove our looks than all the beauty treatments in the
world, and is much less expensive. It may be the
same old temper in the New Year, but that is not to
say that I am going to use it in the same way, and
there may be all the difference in what I do with it
And just because I never have done anything else with
it is not to say that I never can.

Tried Before

And what if you have tried before ? It takes a
woman to try again when things are hopeless and it
seems useless to try. If a woman did not know how
to try again what would she do with the problems of
kitchen floors and Mary's frocks ; to say nothing of
Billy's trousers ? She has been trying for years to keep
those children clean and respectable, and ' trying ' is as
far as she gets. But she keeps on. Most men would

have given up long since. There is a story of Susannah Wesley, John Wesley's mother, who had nineteen children, and taught them all herself, that she repeated one lesson to one of the children so often that her husband grew impatient, as husbands do. ' You have told him that a hundred times already,' he complained. ' Yes, my dear,' she replied, ' but if I had only told him ninety-nine times all my labour would have been lost.' Never mind trying to remember how old you were last birthday, you have not seen ninety-nine New Years yet, so try once more. Maybe this once more will be successful.

All Things New

We cannot do it alone. The arm of flesh will fail us But ' He that sitteth on the throne saith, Behold, I make all things new ' (Rev. xxi. 5). ' New mercies each returning day.' He promises all manner of new things, even a new ' you.' ' A new heart will I give you and a new spirit will I put within you ' (Ezek. xxxvi. 26). He is able to make every day a New Year's Day, and make every New Year a beginning again.

And He never gives in,
So we two shall win,
Jesus and I.

II

THE SPEED LIMIT

IN a letter I had the other day from a young nature-lover he detailed the flowers he had already found in bloom in one place and another and the many welcome signs of approaching Spring and added, ' Even Mr. Hore-Belisha is pushing his thirty miles per hour signs through the earth.' I have heard those signs called many names since they were first erected but I had not before known them included among the flowers that bloom in the Spring. But they are certainly among the things which are among the chief topics of conversation in these days.

I do not want to discuss either their value or their necessity. My purpose is to discuss some other things which they suggest. They suggest, for example, that we should not really lose anything of value if we reduced the speed at which we are living. So many people in these days have an attitude to life which says, ' We don't know where we are going, and we don't know what we are going there for, but we are in a desperate hurry to get there.' The speed of the journey has come to be more important than its purpose or its end. There is a world of suggestion in that story of a fictitious Chinese gentleman in England who was told that the train on which he had just travelled had saved three minutes on the journey. He blandly inquired ' And what shall we do with the three minutes ? '

Time to Live

What have we gained by the craze for speed ? It has invaded the Church. A minister is expected to attend three meetings at three different places in the same evening and to conduct four or five services on a Sunday and attempts to do it. Are we doing more good than we did in the days when the lack of swift transport made that sort of programme impossible ? One is sometimes inclined to copy the Quaker lady who, when a gentleman of numberless activities recited to her the programme of his crowded days, meekly inquired, ' And, pray, friend, when dost thou think ? '

There was a day when the only books which men had opportunity to read were the Bible and the Methodist Hymn Book and, possibly, the *Pilgrim's Progress*. Is the man who has read every best seller and every book of the month for years, who scans three daily papers and two political weeklies any wiser in the real things of life than his grandfather with his scanty library ? Many authorities would deny that even with the added facilities of wireless and the cinema he is any better educated. We are so busy reading the things we must read that we have no time for the things we should read.

> We glimpse all sights from Pole to Pole
>   And glance, and rush, and hurry by ;
> And never once possess our souls
>   Before we die.

It is just as true of the things of the soul. We are too busy to be good. God is crowded out of the lives which are too full of activity. That is why the Groups insist on the importance of the Quiet Time. The Psalmists are always urging men to be patient, to wait on the Lord, to wait till the latter end of the day and see the conclusion of the matter. It is easy to say in our haste, ' All men are liars,' (Ps. cxvi. 11). But at the end we shall be found in the sanctuary paying our vows unto the Lord. If we are too busy to pray, in too much of a hurry to maintain our fellowship with God, it is time we set up a speed limit.

Time to be kind

So many people are in so great a hurry to prosper, in so much haste to succeed that they have no time to consider others, no time to be kind. It was that section of the motoring public which made the imposition of a speed limit necessary. The thirty miles per hour sign says, in effect, ' Do not be in too great a hurry to be considerate of other people.' There used to be a popular saying that road users could be divided between the quick and the dead. It is no longer true. So often it is those who are in most of a hurry who are the soonest dead. The number of lives which are sacrificed every year to the craze for speed is tragic, just because it is such a useless, aimless waste.

' Business is business,' certain people said ; ' if we stopped to consider other people and adapted ourselves to the other fellow's pace we should never get anywhere.' But now many of them are wondering whether kindness and thoughtfulness are not business, also. When we come to the end of the road will our joy and satisfaction come from the remembrance of those whom we helped or those whom we pushed aside ? The Good Samaritan might well have copied the example of the priest and Levite and argued that he had no time to spare for wounded men by the wayside. But when he reached home he must have felt that that deed of kindness was the most profitable bit of business he had done on the whole journey. He was out of pocket but it was a great investment.

Good George Herbert was on his way to Salisbury one day with his instrument under his arm to join some friends who delighted in Chamber music. On the way he found a carter with the wheel of his cart sunk deep in the mire. The Rector stopped to help him, with the result that his clothes were muddy and he was very late for his appointment. ' But,' George Herbert said, as he apologized for his late appearance,

' the memory of it will be music at midnight,' If we are in too much of a hurry to be kind it is time to impose a speed limit.

> ' I made life good,' my Lord will say,
> When we meet at the end of the King's highway—
> ' I mended the children's broken toy,
> I gave the mother back her boy,
> And what did you ? ' my Lord will say,
> When we meet at the end of the King's highway.

III

CLEAN DOORSTEPS

ANYONE who has ever lived in Lancashire knows that Lancashire is the county of clean doorsteps. It is the home of the people who are expert in the art of scrubbing and the use of rubbing stone, and whatever things may be like within, they pride themselves on their doorsteps. It is a typical expression of that British courage which knows that it makes all the difference whether you face difficulty and trial, ' taking it lying down,' or ' standing up to it.' They believe in putting a good face on it. If you are poor you may still be proud, they say, and rubbing stone is cheap, then it only needs a little elbow grease and you have a clean doorstep to show the world. Even if the ornaments have gone from the dresser and there is not much on the table there will still be a clean doorstep.

There are many sayings which recognize the importance of doorsteps. ' If every woman swept her own doorstep, the street would be clean, ' we say. And we say of the woman who minds everyone's business except her own, ' Why does she not clean her own doorstep ? ' And the Bible is full of texts about door-

B

steps. There is the doorstep grace, the threshold blessing, ' the Lord bless thy going out and thy coming in from this time forth and even for evermore ' (Psalm cxxi. 8). And there is the other Psalmist who declared that he ' would rather be a doorkeeper in the house of the Lord,' literally, ' lie on the doorstep of the house of the Lord,' ' than dwell in the tents of wickedness ' (Psalm lxxxiv. 10).

But there are two words which specially bid us to watch our doorsteps. The tragedy of the Story of Cain is that he is haunted by the fear that he will not get a chance. He feels that Abel is God's favourite. So this word of assurance and promise is spoken to Cain : ' If thou doest well shalt thou not be accepted, but if thou doest not well, sin lieth at the door ' (Gen. iv. 7). Give way to sin, God warns him, and it will always be coming back ; you will never have it off your doorstep. We did not think it would be that way. We thought that to give way to it once would be the easiest way to be rid of it. It is just the reverse. Give way to sin once and it will always be waiting for another opportunity ; for some hour when the door is unlatched ; for some hour when you are too tired to argue or resist, ' sin is lying in wait for you, eager to be at you,' Dr. Moffatt translates it.

The doorstep salesman is one of the by-products created by the unemployment problem. You do not know what to do. You feel sometimes that you want to buy to be rid of the persistent canvasser, yet you are afraid that if you do, every other canvasser in the neighbourhood will camp on your doorstep. You have to guard your own doorstep. If dirt is carried over the doorstep it will be carried all over the house, you say, and you know the truth of it.

A clean doorstep means a clean house, that is why you have a doormat and a scraper. A clean threshold means a clean heart, too.

> Each sin has its door of entrance,
>> Keep—that—door—closed !
>> Bolt it tight !
> Just outside the wild beast crouches,
>> In the night.
> Pin the bolt with a prayer,
>> God will fix it there.

The Guest on the Doorstep

The other word about doorsteps comes from the other end of the Bible. The Lord Jesus says : ' Behold, I stand at the door ' (Rev. iii. 20). Have you seen the Lord on the doorstep when you have opened the door in the morning. If you have not seen Him it was not because He was not there, but because you could not see. He does not force his way in. He stands on the doorstep and waits. In Holman Hunt's famous picture, ' The Light of the World,' someone pointed out to the artist that there was no handle on the outside of the door. ' I intended it that way,' he replied, ' the door can only be opened from within.' He came in such great condescension and humility that we did not see Him when He came. He did not say, ' You must,' but, ' Will you ? ' So we did not heed Him on the doorstep, or answer His knock on the door.

In Tolstoy's famous short story *Where Love Is*, Martin, the cobbler, hears a voice which he feels is the voice of the Lord Jesus saying, ' I am coming, Martin,' but the only people who come to his doorstep are the old crossing sweeper, the soldier's wife and baby and the old apple woman. Yet when night has come and Martin is disappointed because the Lord Jesus has not come, he hears the Lord saying ' Inasmuch as you did it unto one of the least of these,' and the cobbler knows that the Lord had really come to his doorstep that day.

What was the impulse to do some fine, lovely thing ; the feeling that you must get away and pray ; the shame that followed the doing of some unworthy, unholy thing, but His knock on the door ; His voice asking meekly and low : May I come in ? Sometimes we turn Him away and refuse to allow Him to enter because we are afraid of the difference which He will make. (Cp. the story of Jerusalem, Luke xiii. 34-5.) But even if the Lord is not answered and the door is not opened we can never drive Him away from our doorstep. Every morning we shall see His footprint in the rubbing stone.

When He sent out the twelve apostles the Lord Jesus commanded them to say, ' The Kingdom of Heaven has come to your door (Matt. x. 7). Do people say that of you ? You have sometimes had cause to say it of others. ' Your coming was a Godsend,' you declare sincerely and gratefully. You felt sweeter happier, cleaner, better because they had come. In literal truth, the Kingdom of Heaven had come to your doorstep. And the Lord Jesus still says, ' as the Father sent Me, even so send I you.' Watch your doorstep and watch what you bring to other people' doorsteps.

IV

A PAIR OF OLD SHOES

ALL women love going to weddings, for some strange
reason which men can never understand, and you
seldom attend a wedding-breakfast without hearing
someone express the wish that the young people will
be ' as comfortable as a pair of old shoes.' That there
may be no doubt about it someone usually manages
to tie an old shoe or two on the bridal carriage, and
because, if the heel of an old shoe happened to hit the
bridegroom he might doubt whether old shoes were as
lucky as they were supposed to be; at all fashionable
weddings they will be pelted with silver shoes. But
the phrase sets one thinking.

Choosing Your Shoes

Choosing a pair of shoes is quite a serious business.
There are so many things to consider. You have to
think what you will wear with them, your shoes must
match your frock. And style is important. You
cannot wear brogues with a georgette frock. It simply
isn't done. Then there is the matter of taste. Mrs.
Smartly may be able to wear something conspicuous in
black and scarlet but it is not your style. And, added
to all these problems, there is the all important question
of comfort and fit. At last, when all these matters are
settled, you ask, ' and how will they wear ? '

The wedding ceremony is over, the great and solemn
vows have been made. Everybody is laughing loudly
because they are feeling a bit choky, the wedding cake

21

is a wreck and the floor is strewn with confetti and crumpled serviettes, all the guests are crowding to the door to see Henry and Edith off ; the air is thick with more confetti ; everyone is telling everyone else, ' they should be happy ; they have had a good send off ' ; then, down in the secret place of the heart Love nudges Experience and adds, ' how will they wear ? '

For folk are like shoes. It is not always the shoes which look nicest in the shop window which are most comfortable on the feet ; and it does not always do to buy your shoes just on the strength of appearances. Will they wear well and grow more comfortable as they grow older ? Henry and Edith are setting out for a long journey. There will be all sorts of roads, rough and smooth, steep and easy. Will they have the comfort of a pair of old shoes for that long road ? For no one who is wise faces a long walk in new shoes, or attempts a steep climb in high heeled shoes which pinch your toes. You hunt out that comfortable pair of old shoes.

And the wear depends on the hidden things. You are almost ashamed to ask the cobbler to repair those shoes again, ' but they are so comfortable,' you plead. He turns them over. ' I can manage,' he says, ' the insole is all right.' But if the insole goes it is a waste of time and money to attempt to do anything with them. How are Henry and Edith going to wear ? It all depends on the insole. And whether you spell it, ' soul ' or ' sole ' it means the same thing.

Creaking Shoes

The next step is creaking shoes. Mr. Jones-Browne-Johnes is on his way up the aisle with the collection plate, ' a stately procession of one,' but his new shoes creak, and Bobby Burt whispers to Sammy Smith, 'creaking shoes. They ain't paid for.' Henry and Edith are back from their honeymoon and are walking on the common road of every day. They have been walking on air while they have been away. Their shoes are pinching a little and squeaking a bit, and down in the secret place of the heart Love whispers to Experience, 'Creaking shoes. They're not paid for.'

Edith is sure Henry does not love her as much as he said he did or he would never be as grumpy as he is sometimes. And Henry cannot understand why Edith is such dull company now that he sees her every day instead of twice a week. She misses the laughter and life of the other girls in the office and he misses his free evenings to spend as he pleased, and there are creaking shoes. But the comfort of old shoes is not something you buy in the shop. Shoes and feet have to grow accustomed to each other. There has to be some give and take. Toes pinch a bit and shoes give a little and they grow comfortable.

The 'Household Hints,' column says: 'The best cure for a pair of creaking shoes is a little sweet oil.' If Henry would hang that over his desk and Edith keep it on her dresser they might well qualify for the Dunmow Flitch. Of course, it is not to be taken literally. Sometimes it is a box of chocolates or a new hat; a box of cigarettes or a silk handkerchief. Oftener it is something left unsaid, a blind eye for things best left unseen; a laugh when you feel like a frown; a smile to hide the tears. It is a very old fashioned remedy. The modern cure for creaking shoes is to change the shoes and then find that the only difference between the old and the new ones is that they pinch in a different place.

Comfortable Shoes

So you come at last to the stage of comfortable shoes. Heels are worn down and toes are rubbed ; they bulge in all the wrong places ; you could never dream of wearing them at a garden party, but they are comfortable on the feet. So you have a vision of Darby and Joan in the House of Happy Dreams at the end of the road. Darby has lost his upright strength that once was so much admired ; Joan's face is as wrinkled as a walnut shell. They have had steep hills to climb, fierce storms with which to battle, dark places through which to grope their way, many a stretch of rough road to face, but they have grown together, fitted in to one another ; and now they are as comfortable as a pair of old shoes.

V

THE MENDING BASKET

THE mending basket is an institution which has never received the honour which is due to it. We are not quite ashamed of it, we should be ashamed if we had no mending basket, but we feel that it is one of the household articles which should be hidden and disguised and kept decently out of sight ; one of the things for whose presence we must apologize if it is ever allowed to come into view. But even if we hide it we are never able to forget it. We may keep it out of sight but we cannot keep it out of mind. We cannot ignore its existence or dismiss its claim on our attention. The vision is before the eyes of our mind : the things which have been pushed into it and piled on top of it ; socks that once had heels and toes and now have them no more ; shirts whose buttons have vanished, whose collarbands are only a memory, whose cuffs are mere fringes. There are little trousers that need a large patch and vests that require a good many darns. It is no wonder that the mending basket overflows.

Not Worth Mending

Some things are there which scarcely seem worth mending, they are so old and worn. But they have been ours so long that something like affection for them has grown up in us. They show the rub of much service and traces of the wear and strain of everyday, but they have been good servants and there is a feeling that it would not be quite fair to discard them now. So, even though others would write them down as worthless and useless they find their way to the mending basket and we make an effort to find some way to make them last a little longer.

And some things have had hard usage and have not been treated fairly. They are in such a state that you scarcely know where to begin. Buttons have been broken and wrenched off. Damage has been done which was not just wear and tear. They have been cut by someone's recklessness and folly, torn where they were caught on thorns and nails. They are much too good to throw away but you almost despair of mending them. You feel a measure of sympathy for them, almost as though they were alive. You say what a shame it is that decent clothes should be treated in such a fashion ; how good they would be if only they had been treated properly ; and with that sympathy and care in your heart you sit down to mend them.

Mending is not the easiest job in the world. Many a woman declares with deep conviction ' I would rather make than mend, any day,' and we all have a proper admiration for those specialists who ask us to allow them to perform ' invisible mending. It is a great art if you are really able to fulfil that promise ; to darn the hole so that you cannot see where the hole was made ; to patch the rent where the thorns caught so skilfully that the damage will never show ; to repair the worn garment until it is once more ' as good as new,' that is an art which deserves all our appreciation and all our praise. To have patched up something that was almost past patching so that it will last a while longer is a service splendidly worth while. It is not easy to remember it when we face that piled-up mending basket. Is that old, worn thing worth all the work and skill and thought ? It has been patched so often, mended so many times before. But we patch it again. It will last a bit longer.

Worn out Souls

Folk wear out just as clothes and stockings do, and we all find ourselves at last in the Lord's mending basket. Patience is almost worn out ; hope will scarcely stand the strain ; tempers and nerves get frayed and ragged ; they all need mending and renewing. Some people's souls are getting a bit thin and worn. They need darning and strengthening. That threadbare place of patience and hope is getting very thin ; it needs patching underneath with the strength which God supplies through His eternal Son. The Lord takes up the needle of His love and sets to work and the needle goes in and out, over and under, weaving the new, strong threads of grace into the worn place of our endurance and desire. And the life that was so poor and worn that it only seemed fit for the rummage sale is made serviceable and secure and strong again. We come with our tattered faith, and our frayed nerves, and our worn-out patience, and our threadbare hopes and we go our way with strength renewed, mended in soul.

Peter was suffering from badly frayed nerves. Things had rubbed and fretted and worn until there was scarcely a fibre left. It was not surprising that when a sudden strain came the frayed place gave way and there was a great gaping rent. Most of us would have said that that was the end. A character such as that was beyond hope of repair, nor was it worth bothering with. It was of no use to attempt to mend it. If you made an effort and mended that weak place you could be sure that another weak place would develop before long, and there would be a fresh failure and a greater rent. It would only be a waste of thought and strength to attempt to mend a character as frayed and weak as Peter's had proved itself to be.

The Lord Jesus thought differently. He set about the task of mending. ' Simon, Son of Jonas, lovest thou Me ? ' The sharp, smooth needle of love passed in and began to draw the frayed, torn edges of hope and love together. Threads of sympathy and under-standing and love crossed the rent in character. Courage and patience were all worn through and had to be re-woven. Over and under, under and over, the needle went in and out. ' Simon, son of Jonas, lovest thou Me ? ' And now the pattern of the darn began to show clear. ' Feed my sheep.' Very carefully, very tenderly, the needle went to and fro. In a little while the rent had been mended. The frayed nerves, the threadbare patience, the outworn courage had all been re-woven.

' Lord, Thou knowest all things. Thou knowest that I love Thee ! ' ' Feed my sheep ! ' Peter was strong and whole again. Mended ! That worn and tattered life had been made whole again.

He is just the same to-day and when you feel that nerves are getting frayed and patience is wearing thin ; when you feel that you are getting so utterly worn out that you simply cannot go on much longer ; when you have been treated badly, and love and faith are torn and rent, and seem almost beyond repair, just go to Him. He will darn the thin places and strengthen the weak places and mend the torn places and do it all so skilfully and well that things will really be made good. He specializes in invisible mending and nothing is too hard for the Lord.

VI

A PAIR OF SPECTACLES

A FRIEND of mine, who suffered from persistent tooth-ache was sent by her dentist to consult a doctor, but she was naturally surprised when the doctor sent her to an oculist and declared that the only thing which would cure her toothache was a fresh pair of spectacles. The advice was not as foolish as it sounded. Nerves re-act upon each other in a curious fashion, and it was soon proved that eye-strain was causing toothache. In all manner of ways in these times we are finding that a pair of spectacles will make all the difference to physical and mental well-being.

Unfortunately, we are much slower to recognize the fact that mental vision has as great an influence on mental and moral health as physical vision has on physical health. One man looks at the world through rose-coloured spectacles, another sees it through smoked glasses, but neither sees the world as it really is. Each man's vision is distorted by the spectacles he wears.

Change Your Glasses

So, if you are suffering from the blues, change your glasses. You will find that the blueness is not in the world at which you are looking but in the glasses you are wearing. ' You cannot be optimistic if you have misty optics,' says a card in the window of my optician, and I know he is right. There is all the difference between looking at the world through a golden haze of hope or the dark mists of despair. This world is not a bad place if you learn to look at it in the right way. Do you know the old jingle verse ?

> This world that we are living in
> Is mighty hard to beat,
> You get a thorn with every rose,
> But aren't the roses sweet ?

Some people spend all their time counting the thorns, and prick their fingers in the process. Wiser people forget the thorns in remembering how sweet the roses were. In a recent popular film, the central character is filled with bitterness against a world where the vision of the beauty of the flowers is mocked by the thought of his own crippled life, until one day he picks up a pair of field glasses and looks at the world through them, and discovers that there is love and kindness, sacrifice and courage in the world, and a chance for him to show helpfulness and kindness, patience and faith. He was the same man, with the same crippling limitations, living in the same world, all that had happened was that he was looking at the world through different glasses.

What of the Church ?

And, equally, if you are getting to despair of the world of men and things—change your glasses. There is a legend of an old father of the Christian Church that he dreamed of the Church as an old, feeble woman, too infirm to stand, collapsed upon a chair. But as he looked he saw the skin of the age-withered face grow young and beautiful, and the Church became a splendid figure, standing strong and vigorous on her feet. When he looked again she had changed even more wonderfully, and had become a majestic figure seated in royal splendour on an immovable throne. And an angel standing beside him said : ' She looked old and infirm only because you had grown worldly and broken and unexpectant. God in His pity sent some faith into your heart and you saw that His Church is greater than you had believed ! He increased your own courage and you realized she is invincible. It was not she, but you, that was at fault.'

This world is not lying in the power of the evil one but in the loving care of the God and Father of our Lord Jesus Christ, and if you are not convinced of the truth of that fact it is a sign that your glasses need changing. Dean Inge once described prophets as people whose mission it is to teach men to see the world through new glasses, and went on to say that the secret of their unpopularity is that men feel that it is so much more comfortable to continue using the old ones. It means so much adjustment of thought and life when you see the world through different glasses.

There is a delightful story told of Mrs. George Macdonald. Ruskin was passing through a time of great spiritual darkness, and wrote his friend George Macdonald, saying that if he felt it was possible for him to go direct to the Heavenly Father, the first thing he would say to Him would be, ' What have you been teasing me like this for ? Were there *no* toys in the cupboard you could have shown me—but the one I can't have ? ' George Macdonald sent the letter on to his wife, and she replied : ' How dreadfully sad it is. Can he be quite sure that God opened the cupboard door and showed him this best toy ? Might he not have seen it through a chink or by looking at it when the door was opened to others ? Because the Father has other children and He lets us look at each other's toys.' If only Ruskin could have borrowed Mrs. Macdonald's spectacles.

What is Success ?

Likewise, if you despair of other people, change your glasses. ' I always speak of people as I find them,' we sometimes boast. That may be perfectly true. Probably it is. But even so what we find in people largely depends on how we look at them and what we look for, it depends on the glasses we wear. Rudyard Kipling, in one of his earlier poems, ' Tommy Atkins,' has a perfect illustration of this principle.

For it's Tommy this, an' Tommy that, an' ' Chuck him out, the brute ! '
But it's ' Saviour of 'is country,' when the guns begin to shoot.

It all depends on whether you look at people through the spectacles of pride or the glasses of love and appreciation. Mr. A. C. Benson tells the story of an unsuccessful man. ' He never had time to do himself

justice. He was always too busy doing things for othe
people. He would do things for you as carefully, a
punctually as if his own reputation depended on i
He is a middle-aged man with hundreds of friends an
a small income. He lives in a poky house in th
suburbs and works harder than any man I know.
one meets him he has the same, beautiful, tired smi
and fifty things to ask one, all about oneself. I can
describe what good it does one to meet him. What
difference he makes to so many people and what
beautiful thing his life is ! The other day I met
cousin of his, a prosperous man of business, " Yes, poo
Harry goes on in his feckless way. It's all very we
to be at everyone's beck and call, but it doesn't pay "

Doesn't it ? It all depends on the spectacles yo
wear as you look at life.

VII

WHAT SHALL WE WEAR ?

THE question of dress is one which never loses it
interest. Whatever shop windows we may pass withou
a second glance, the windows which display things t
wear always attract us and win our attention. W
all pretend to be superior to it, claim that clothe
really have little or no interest for us, and so on, but i
our more candid hours we all recognize that clothe
have a very great influence upon us and possess a
importance which cannot be wholly forgotten. W
do feel an added sense of responsibility and well-bein
when we are well dressed. We all like the feeling tha

our clothes are attractive and appropriate, and we
are more careful of speech and behaviour when we are
wearing our best clothes.

Clothes Make the Man

A famous firm of clothiers have long used a poster
with the legend, ' Clothes make the man.' At first
sight the poster is a picture of Napoleon standing in his
familiar attitude with legs wide spread and his hand
thrust into his breast. But a second glance reveals
that the figure only consists of the clothes. It is, of
course, an advertiser's exaggeration, but clothes do
make a difference, and to women even more than men.
You see a lady coming along the street and she looks
very attractive. But when she comes near enough for
you to be able to see clearly you find that she is anything but attractive. The attraction was wholly in
the clothes she wore, not in herself at all. So the
question of ' What shall we wear ? ' really is important,
and most of us need all the help that dressmakers can
give us if we are to make the best of ourselves.

All this is not to say that people are to be judged by
their clothes. There are as many sinners in silk as
there are saints in homespun and, what is less often
asserted, that there are many saints in silk and many
sinners in homespun. Yet few people can afford to
completely ignore the question of clothes. It is true
that there are people who can afford to ignore all the
claims of dress, disgracefully dressed dukes and shabby
millionaires, but it is only dukes and millionaires who
can dare to be so regardless of the outward appearances
by which most of us are judged. They may be able to
wear anything they please because, for one reason or
another, they are beyond criticism, but the rest of us

c

have to study, 'what will be worn this season,' and follow the lead of the people who create the fashion.

There was a day, of course, when a man's clothes were the sign of his profession. The monk still retains his habit and the nun her coif and, in less noticeable ways, the butcher still wears his blue smock, the chef his cap, and the parson his collar. There was a day when the Quaker was known by his broad-brimmed hat, and his wife by her dress of sober grey, and in some good Methodist homes they still treasure the long black shawl and the black bonnet with its beautifully pleated frill which was the badge of the Methodist woman of an earlier generation. Clothes had more than a small significance then and the dress was the symbol of the character. The apparel oft proclaimed the man.

Clothes and Character

One of the most interesting things in the Book of Revelation is to see the significance which is given to clothes. The woman who is the symbol of the power of evil, is clothed with purple and scarlet, and decked with gold and precious stones and pearls, and the woman who is the symbol of humanity is clothed with the sun with the moon under her feet, and upon her head a crown of twelve stars. Most familiar of all is the symbol of the white robes, the sign of those who have overcome and washed their robes and made them white in the blood of the Lamb. But there is this significant thing that while these white robes are given to them, they can neither be purchased nor earned ; they are still fashioned by the wearers. ' The white linen is the righteousness of saints.'

The meaning of it is the thing we practise in everyday life. Beautiful clothes are attractive, no one denies it. We all like to feel well-dressed, and we should all like to dress a little better than we do. We all know when we are wearing clothes that suit us, which bring out our best points and hide our deficiencies, and we all feel a little more sure of ourselves and face the world with a little more confidence if we feel that we are looking our best. But, when all that has been said, we each know that what we are in ourselves matters more than the most beautiful garments we can put on ; we know that in the long run a well dressed soul is vastly more important than a beautifully clothed body. What we are matters more than how we look.

If only people's clothes corresponded to their characters what a strange world it would be ; what an awful world it would be. If only the people with beautiful souls and characters were allowed to wear beautiful dresses, there would be some beautiful dresses brightening the dreariness of some dingy slums and there would be some shabby dresses looking strangely out of place in palaces and mansions. Suppose that every nasty thought meant a stain upon our clothes and every gloomy doubt a smudge ; if every dirty thought meant a dirty mark, and every greedy desire was like the smear of sticky fingers on our garments what should we look like ? Life would be impossible if our clothes really revealed what we are instead of disguising it.

The Dress Length of Character

But that is exactly what is happening to us here and is being prepared for us hereafter. ' The white linen is the righteousness of saints,' something we are weaving on the loom of time like a weaver fashions a dress-length of material for you to wear. The fabric may well be so fine and delicate that it seems incredible, but it is none the less true that it was woven thread by thread, one thread at a time passing through the threads upon the beam ; bright threads and dark ones, shining threads and gloomy ones, and all alike helping to make the pattern of the dress you wear. Characters are woven just as dress-lengths are. We cannot choose the beams. They are put on the loom for us. But we can choose what we weave into them.

And when the dress is finished we must wear it. It is part of ourselves. It is the only self which will last and abide. What shall we wear ? The question is always with us. We want something suitable something in which we look our best ; something which expresses the best side of our character and personality Often we complain, ' I should like something better but that is the best I can afford.' But do let us remember that day by day we are weaving the dress-leng tho character which we must wear through all eternity, tha what we are matters more than what we put on ; fo some day we shall drop our bodies like we step out o an old, worn-out dress, and the character we hav woven will be ours for evermore.

VIII

EASY CHAIRS

HAVE you noticed how furniture fashions have change in recent years. In the old days the important questio was, will it last ? Now the question is, will it be con fortable ? People used to believe in chairs with har seats and straight backs. They denied themselves the luxury of lounging. Life was real and earnest, even if you sat down you still had to remember that, and you must not rest too much. Do you remember the old front room with horsehair furniture, cold and slippery, which antimacassars made more slippery still? Do you remember the round table with its wool mats and wax fruits and its books in formal places at proper intervals? It was a place to possess but not to enjoy. To-day things have changed completely and we look for a Chesterfield suite, deep in cushions, made for lounging and ease.

The truth, probably, is somewhere midway. We must do our work; but we do need easy chairs when our work is done; chairs which will hold us in comfort and ease, chairs whose embrace will be soft and pleasant, where weary limbs and tired nerves and strained muscles can be rested. And when we look at the very modern fashion for something very massive with never an attractive curve anywhere, or something very cold and severe in steel tubing, the question in our hearts is 'Will it be comfortable?' We want a chair in which we can rest, and feel rested. For, while some of this furniture may be very up-to-date, it is like gas fires and electric radiators, they are very efficient, but there is no comfort in them.

Everlasting Love

Here is a comfortable easy chair, everlasting love. It is not enough to rest limbs and muscles; we need to rest minds and hearts. The real cause of our breakdowns is not the work but the worry. You make up your mind that you will stop thinking too much and too long but the more you try the worse it is. It is easy enough for the doctor to say that all you need is rest, but how are you going to get it ? If you sit down with your feet up before last night's ashes and think of the pile of washing waiting to be done and the floor that has to be scrubbed it does you more harm than good, because you are worrying all the time.

' Cast thy burden upon the Lord and He shall sustain thee ' (Psalm lv. 22). It sounds just magic and mystery, but it works. Just to remember that you are not bearing the burden alone, not even the burden of Jim's tantrums and the week's washing and the baby's teething ; that everlasting love is something which is concerned with the little things of everyday life, which cares for your problems and your needs, is to learn one of the great secrets of rest and renewal. John says that the Lord Jesus manifested His glory when He used His Divine power to save a girl's wedding breakfast from being spoiled. (John ii. 11.)

Just Pray

Can you sit down in the easy chair of prayer ? If someone comes in when things are at their worst someone who cares and understands, and you have a talk, what a difference it makes. The burden is still there, the problem is still unsolved ; but you feel better. The burden does not drag quite as much, the problem is not so overpowering ; you have renewed your faith that there will be a way out. ' I feel better now,' you say to Mrs. Cheery as she goes. You feel as though you had sat down for an hour in a comfortable arm chair with your feet up and had a real rest.

That is what prayer does for you. It is not just a method of getting your own way and getting things you had set your heart on ; it is a quiet fellowship

with Someone who loves and knows and understands.
' Come unto Me, all ye that are weary and heavy laden
and I will rest you ' (Matt. xi. 28). You are no longer
lonely and friendless and misunderstood. Do not shut
Christ out from your working hours, do not wait for
the end of the day, but when things are getting on top
of you ; just pray. ' He'll put His loving arms around
you.'

It is a wonderful old chair. Children have knelt
about it ; the tears of heart-broken women have
stained it, strong men have battered it as they have
stormed the gates of heaven and all have added something to it. Everybody has this easy chair. You may
not have much furniture ; nothing that would fetch
much in the market. But the Lord Jesus is not too
proud to visit you. His nature and His name is
Love. No home is too poor, no place too ugly for
Him to come into it. Ugliness and gloom cannot
shut Him out. Where He is most needed, there
He is most near. Sit down in that easy chair and
talk to Him and see the difference it makes.

And Praise

There is another easy chair just like it on the other
side of the hearth, the easy chair of praise. The
Psalmists and prophets knew that chair and loved it.
' Though the fig tree shall not flourish,' they sang,
' yet will I rejoice in the Lord ' (Habakkuk iii. 17-18).
Job would not cast it out though his wife urged him to
do so. (Job ii. 9.) ' Though He slay me, yet will I trust
in Him ' (Job. xiii. 15). Our Lord Himself knelt at
the other chair and sat in this one as the darkness
gathered about Him. ' And when they had sung a

hymn, they went out to the Mount of Olives ' (Mark xiv. 26). And the hymn they sang that night was, ' O give thanks unto the Lord, for He is good ' (Psalm cxviii.). It is a wonderful old chair. If you sit in it for a while you rise up rested, brave and strong. And it never goes out of fashion. Our fathers and mothers rested in it and we do well to sit in it, too.

IX

A TALK ABOUT TALKING AND TALKERS

EVERYBODY can talk, especially if you can get them started. The trouble with most people is to know when to stop. But even the most silent and tongue-tied people grow eloquent when you set them off on their own topic. It may not be your topic, it may be golf or operations, but they keep on talking so that you cannot get a word in, and at the end of an hour's solid talking they say, ' what a lovely conversation we have had ! ' It is like that famous story of Carlyle and Emerson sitting together by the fireside, smoking, for a whole evening, never exchanging a word, until, as one rose to go, the other said, ' Man, it's been a great time.' But they were men, and, as all the world knows, men cannot talk ; at least, they say so.

But talk may be the greatest thing in the world, especially preaching, which after all, is nothing but a public talk. The subject of the talk is the secret of its greatness. Do you remember how something which someone said in an hour of darkness was like a lamp lit in a dark room, and the place that was full of terrify-ing shadows suddenly became a place of security and peace. It was only a word of warning or appeal in the hour of your temptation, when your feet had well-nigh slipped, but it steadied your heart and held you up. A quiet talk with an understanding friend saved your faith in the hour of your despair. Just talk, it was nothing more ; but it saved you.

Only Talk

It is only talk ; but it may be the worst and most harmful thing in the world. ' Only talk,' but a woman's good name is stolen and her character is stained so deeply that years afterwards the marks are still there. ' If only I could forget what she said,' but you cannot and life will never be the same again. Words cause wounds which never heal ; put poison into the blood which can never be worked out. That is the best and the worst of talking. It can do so much good ; it may do so much harm. Do you remember Will Carleton's ballad, ' The Settler's Story,' of the harm done by idle words, and the moral he draws ?

> Boys flying kites haul in their white-winged birds,
> You can't do that when you are flying words,
> Careful with fire, is good advice, we know,
> Careful with words, is ten times doubly so,
> Thoughts unexpressed may sometimes fall back dead ;
> But God Himself can't kill them when they're said.

St. James draws three pictures of the power of the tongue. It is like a bit in the horse's mouth, by which a child can guide a great animal ; like the rudder of a ship, by which the whole vessel is turned about ; like a fire kindled by a spark. A cigarette end is dropped, and a great building goes up in flames and many lives are lost ; or it drops in the dry grass and a whole countryside is devastated.

> Careful with fire is good advice, we know ;
> Careful with words is ten times doubly so.

We cannot help talking, but we can help what we talk about, seek for the good and avoid the perils. Ella Wheeler Wilcox's verses ; ' Talk happiness. Talk faith. Talk health,' might be quoted.

Talk Appreciation and not Criticism

Jeremy Taylor writes of people who spend their days gathering a handful of thorns to sit upon, and talk about the discomfort of it. Americans lay a good deal of emphasis on what they call ' boosting ' their home town. They praise it and advertise it wherever they go. English people seldom do. We are too conscious of its limitations and deficiencies, ' I would give anything to get away from it.' And six months after you have gone you are wishing you could return. Every town has something in it for which we may be glad.

So with our homes. They may not be mansions or palaces, but it makes a wonderful difference if we talk appreciation instead of criticism. I heard of a woman who lived in a dull sunless room, who rejoiced that she could see the sun shine on the houses opposite, and of a philosopher who always boasted of his garden, and at last took his friends to see it. When they remarked on its cramped narrowness, he smiled and said, ' See how high it is.' Things are better for us if we praise them to others. Every house has some defect, but it has some excellencies, too.

It is the same with people ; even husbands. All

the perfect husbands are dead. They were too good to live, but no one knew it until it was too late. Every man is too trying for words in some way or other. But even the most difficult have some good points and they are worth looking for and talking about. When people criticized Mr. Wiggs's lack of fine features, his wife declared that she would no more dream of thinking of his nose without Mr. Wiggs than that she would think of Mr. Wiggs without his nose.

Nor is it only true of husbands. If we had had the making of some of the people whom we know how differently we should have made them. But we have to take them as they are and make the best of them. If you must criticize do it with sadness and not with glee. How easy it is to rub our hands over someone else's fall. ' I never liked that woman. I always thought there was something shifty about her.' But ' love is never glad when others go wrong. Love rejoices not in iniquity.' We are followers of Him who was the Friend of the outcast and the sinner, the people for whom no one could find a good word to say. Talk happiness, appreciation, kindness and these things will come back to you. ' With what judgement you judge, you shall be judged ; and the measure you deal to others will be dealt out to you.'

X

PEOPLE WE CANNOT SPARE

HAVE you ever been in a meeting when they have debated the old question, ' Who shall be thrown out of the balloon ? ' An imaginary balloon is in difficulties, and one of the passengers must be thrown out to save the lives of the others. The passengers include, for example, a poet, a scientist, a farmer, and you debate which of the three can be most easily spared by the community. It is capable, of course, of endless variations and of endless debate. But to-day let us look at the portraits of three or four people whom none of us would be willing to spare.

Mr. Punch : the Humorist

If you praise the man who makes two blades of grass grow where only one grew before, what honour will you give to the man who makes two smiles twinkle where only one, or possibly none, twinkled before ? How should we get through the dark days of life without the humorist. The Englishman never takes things so seriously that he cannot smile. When, in the war years, Germany sang a hymn of hate, Englishmen took it as a great joke, We invented ' Ole Bill ' with his ' better 'ole.' And, however bad the outlook, and however great the problems, thanks be to God for the gift of seeing the funny side of it.

But many people have an idea that humour is not quite religious. In *God in Everything*, Parson John is asked whether it is right to read *Punch*, and replies that he is convinced that God helps to write it every week. Oliver Wendell Holmes satirizes the people who spend their days preparing for a smileless heaven, and who would be inclined to cut off a kitten's tail if they caught the animal playing with it. But the Bible says that in Heaven there will be no more tears, not, no more smiles. ' A saint who is sad is a very poor saint.' So let us thank God for every man who writes

a clean joke or draws a funny sketch. How unbearable
life would be without humour.

Mr. Cheeryman : the Optimist

The boy who is credited with the statement that the
optimist is the man who looks after your eyes, and the
pessimist is the man who attends to your feet was not
so far from the truth. The optimist is the one who
looks up and sees the stars ; the pessimist is he who,
looking down, only sees the mud and the puddles.
The one man sees hope and promise, the other depression and despair. When Mr. Cheeryman hears the
familiar announcement in the weather forecast of a
depression off the coast of Ireland he remarks to Mary,
' I'm thankful that I don't live there ' ; and even
when she complains of a flooded cellar, he immediately
throws up his hat and declares that he had always
wanted to keep ducks.

If there is no jam to-day he remembers the jam
they had yesterday, and anticipates jam to-morrow,
and sometimes finds that to-day's bread is not so very
dry. His good cheer is infectious. When Paul and
Silas sang praises to God in the jail at Philippi the
prisoners heard. They always do. It is Mr. Cheeryman
who, when things are at their worst, says that he has
faced worse things than this, and has been brought
through, and that the Lord who has brought him as
far as this will not abandon him but will see him through
to the end. Remember, it was in the darkest hour of
human history that the Lord Jesus said, ' Let not your
heart be troubled, ye believe in God.'

Mr. Help : the Serviceable

Do you ever give God thanks that there is so much in this world which is needing to be done and that there are so many ways in which helpful and serviceable things may be done ? What would life be like if there was nothing to do for other people ; no one's burdens to lift, no one's sorrows to comfort ; no one's trials to bear ? Life would scarcely be worth living if there was not something to do for others. John Bunyan has given us the portrait of ' A man called Help,' who lived hard by the Slough of Despond and helped out those pilgrims who were unfortunate enough to fall into the mire of that place.

It was not the pleasantest place in which to build a desirable villa-residence ; but what would have happened if he had moved away ? How many pilgrims would have been swallowed up in the mire but for his guidance and his strong arm to rescue them. How great a debt we owe to Mr. Help and his friends. He came when he was most needed and gave help to those who most required it. Small, prompt payments, someone says, are better than the largest promissory notes ; especially in the matter of help.

> We shall do so much in the years to come,
> But what have we done to-day ?
> We shall give our gifts in a princely sum ;
> But what have we given to-day ?

Mr. Nobody : the Unknown

Of course, it is Mr. Nobody who breaks all the pots and spills all the ink, and leaves all the dirty footmarks on the clean floors. But how great a debt we owe to him. When you buy a four and eleven silk frock, you know that it was not cut out by Mr. Marks and made up by Mr. Spencer; but that it was the work of Mr. Nobody or his daughter. It was Mr. Nobody who grew the potatoes and tomatoes and gathered the plums you had for dinner. He sweeps the roads and lights the streets for us, drives the bus, and prints our daily paper. It was Mr. Nobody who first thought of tinned fruit, and invented artificial silk. He is that unknown man whose thought and labour and service make all our life possible. No one remembers him, no one praises him, but what could we do without him. These are some of the people whom we cannot spare.

XI

PEOPLE WE COULD EASILY SPARE

THERE are some people whom we could easily spare from our own little world; at least, we think we could do very well without them. One is not quite so sure after a little consideration. We are all convinced that we could do without wasps, especially at picnics, but too few wasps would mean too many flies, so the authorities say. If we had nothing in the world but nice, pleasant people who always saw the best side of us and always said pleasant, comfortable things, how happy we should be. But would the world be better without some of the people whom we would gladly spare? Artemus Ward, the famous American humorist, declared that his enthusiasm for the Civil War was so great that he would willingly sacrifice all his wife's relations. Whom would we gladly sacrifice?

Mrs. Grump : who always sees the dark side

She always sees the dark side of circumstances. If
it is fine to-day she reminds you that it rained yesterday, or prophesies that it will rain to-morrow. Her
corn or her rheumatism is more reliable than the
weather forecasts. She has a son who takes after her.
Things in his line of business are always going from bad
to worse. He loses money every week. In spite of it he
still manages to keep up appearances and bought a new
motor car last season. But he always says that he
cannot keep going much longer. When Jim comes home
worn out, miserable and snappy, and you ask him what
has happened, he tells you he has met John Grump, and
that accounts for his mood. It is creditably reported
that Mrs. Grump was perfectly miserable even at her
wedding. She was very doubtful about the whole
proceeding and hesitated a full minute before she said,
' I will.' It turned out badly, but she would have been
disappointed if it had not done so. We could spare Mrs.
Grump.

She always sees the dark side of character, and
that is worse. There is little good left in anyone's
reputation when she has done with them. If she has
not found out anything bad about them she is hopeful
that she soon will do so. Not that there is much need
for her to find out anything ; a few wishes and hints
and nods are sufficient, or a suggestion ' If I was to say
all I know.' Mrs. Grump does not really know anything but she is hopeful. ' I knew a woman before
who looked just like her. She did not take me in. I
knew that still waters run deep. You mark my words,
we shall hear something about her before long,' and
Mrs. Grump passes by looking wise.

And she always tells you how ill you look. You feel you ought to be able to confess that the doctor is calling in a specialist, just to satisfy her. She is really disappointed, and does not altogether believe you if you tell her that there is nothing worse amiss with you than pork pie for supper. Whatever you do, do not copy Mrs. Grump. Look for the glad things for other people's sake and for your own. Look for the good things, seek something to praise and admire. You will get more joy out of life, so will others.

Mrs. Fretful : who is very touchy

Mrs. Fretful's great trouble is that she has corns. Now an occasional corn can be understood and forgiven. But Mrs. Fretful's feet are all corns, and they are so big that you cannot help stepping on them. They always seem to be getting in other people's way. You try to avoid them, but the harder you try the more clumsy you are. And they are such horribly sensitive corns. You only need to touch them to set them hurting. In fact, you are not even sure that you did touch them, you only came near them, and Mrs. Fretful screamed in agony. You never heard such a fuss ; and all about a trifle ; that someone approached one of her many corns.

And she does not get over it. She has so good a memory that even Mr. Pelman could not improve it. If you pass her in the street, or smile at her story when you should have sighed, she will remember it for fifteen years and a day. You have spoken to her a hundred times since ; you have always sympathized and understood ; but she has never got over it. She is always a little distant and reserved, always reminding you of what happened, without mentioning it.

D

The trouble is that her touchiness is so one-sided
If only she was as careful of other people's feelings as
she is of her own, we could understand and forgive
But she never seems to remember that other people
are touchy, too. Her great, clumsy feet are alway
treading on other people's toes. We know that her
corns make her walk clumsily, but she never apologizes
She feels that we should apologize for allowing our fee
to be in her way. She only does what is right ; a
least, it is right in her own eyes, and she only acts a
one in her position could be expected to act. If onl
we could send Mrs. Fretful to some spiritual chiropodis
what a difference it would make. We would gladl
spare her for a few days, or even for a few weeks, i
only we thought she could come back cured.

If you want to be wanted ; if you are anxious to b
included in the happy fellowship of the people wh
cannot be spared, be among those who pass throug
life looking for the bright side, seeing the best of th
circumstances of life ; seeing the best of men an
women about you ; be more considerate of othe
people's troubles than you are of your own ; have
good memory for the kindnesses and the complimen
of life and a poor memory for the injuries and slights
then you will find that you will always be welcom
and people will be glad of your company.

XII

SHOP-WINDOW GAZING

WE ERECT monuments to all sorts of people to-day and our children will remove them to-morrow because the people whose memory they were intended to make immortal have been forgotten and the statues are hindering the traffic. But so many of the people who most deserve statues never get them. Surely there should be a statue of the man who taught us to drink tea—what would life be without it ?—and a colourful memorial to the man who first combined strawberries and cream. We should keep before us the immortal memory of the inventor of stainless cutlery and delivered us from the drudgery of knife cleaning, and there should be a memorial to the inventor of the modern shop-window for all the pleasure he has given us.

Do you remember the old shop-window with its small, dingy panes ; where brushes and bacon, biscuits and blacking, bullseyes and boots, buckets and bottles of pickles all mingled in one glorious, smelly confusion ? But the modern display man is an artist. He takes a bolt of silk, unfolds it in a long, shimmering sweep, drapes it and spreads it, and says, ' You would look lovely dressed in that ; come and buy it ! ' Or he shows you a knit suit the colour of newly-opened, green leaves, with a belt of cowslip yellow. ' Come and wear this,' he says, ' and you would look as beautiful as a meadow in Spring when the grass is growing and the first flowers are opening.' In Autumn he puts out something as warm and magnificent as the flame of a wood fire. ' If you must grow old,' he whispers,

' wear something like this and grow old beautifully.'
When life is grey and dull and skies are cloudy, we go
and look at the shop-windows. It costs nothing, and
you are cheered by seeing all the lovely things there
are in the world.

The Perils of It

The question in our minds most often is, who wears
the things in the shop-windows ? You look at furniture
which appears to have been planned in a nightmare and
designed to produce a maximum of discomfort and you
cannot imagine anyone living with it. But somebody
will. ' Copies of priceless antiques,' the showcard
says ; and you feel that the only virtue they can claim
is that they are antiques ; you prefer something cosy
and comfortable. Who wears those very fashionable
frocks and the shoes with toes so sharp and heels so
high that you could walk on the tip of one toe in them
and the hats that look as though they would never
fetch two-pence in a Jumble Sale.

There are mysteries in shop-windows. Why should
it only be necessary to label some atrocity ' Exclusive
Paris model. £2. 2s. Not on sale till nine a.m. to
morrow,' to make people fight for it ? And why is a
man's suit always priced at £5. 5s. and his wife's a
£4. 19. 11¾ ; as if the bundle of hairpins, ' your change
madam,' was of any use now-a-days ? If only you
could buy all the things you set your heart on in the
shop-windows you could make a sensation.

The Privilege of It

Would you really be any happier if you could buy
the shop-window display ? The people who slide past
in great motors huddled in fur coats seldom look happy

somehow. They do not wear their hearts on their
sleeves but if they did, would you find much satisfaction
there ? If you asked them what they got their happiness
out of they would tell you that it is not out of the car
and the fur coat and the shop-window ; but out of the
fact that there is someone who loves them and who is
kind and thoughtful because they love. They have a
few friends whom they can trust and to whom they can
gossip, and a little child or two who are worth more
than all the jewels in Bond Street. ' A man's life con-
sisteth not in the abundance of the things which he
possesseth,' nor does his happiness.

David Grayson says that he found a whole lot of
happiness in looking at the shop-windows and seeing
what a lot of things there were in the world which he
did not have to bother with, for which he had no desire
and did not want. You remember the poster of the
' Bisto Kids,' turning up their noses at the Rolls-
Royce which they passed in their soap box. ' Godli-
ness with contentment is great gain.' James Smetham,
the great Methodist artist, was urged to go to the Con-
tinent for a holiday for the sake of his art. ' My difficulty,' he said, ' is to appreciate our little back garden,
our copper beech, our weeping ash, our little nailed-up
rose tree and twisting yellow creepers.'

That is the privilege of shop-window gazing, to come
home with the memory of all the beauty and splendour
and still be content. Can you live in a smoky, industrial
town and see the splendour of the sky when the sun
goes down and out of the smoke and grime make
pictures more splendid than the Royal Academy ever
saw, the glory of God's shop-window ? Said Dr. Dale,
a generation ago, ' Do not complain of your want of
riches, of your hard work, of your want of distinction.

Glory in the greatness of your position as sons of God
and heirs of eternal blessedness. Think what you are.
The Eternal God loves you with a love as warm as that
which He has for the richest and most eminent of your
Christian brethren. You are as dear to Him as if you
had the estate of a duke. You are His child, glory in
your high estate. You are poor, but you are not at
home. You are on a journey, on your way to the home
that God has prepared for you. Even princes do not
wear their robes and crowns when they are travelling,
nor do rich men carry their wealth with them. You
too, are rich enough at home, and you are on your
way there.' This world, with all its love and beauty
and glory is God's shop-window ; but it is not all in
the shop-window. ' Eye hath not seen, nor ear heard,
neither hath it entered into the heart of man, the
things which God hath prepared for them that love
Him ' (Cor. ii. 9).

XIII

I. O. U.

DEBTS are seldom pleasant topics for discussion. To
pay as you go may be the secret of a quiet mind but
not everyone believes it. We all know the people who
are quite ready to pawn the front room furniture to
find money for a holiday ; or pay an unpleasant visit
to the gentleman who declares that nothing in the
world would give him so much pleasure as to lend you
£20 for the same good purpose. But they are not the
people for whom we have any great admiration

whose example we are at all anxious to copy. Shakespeare was as wise as he usually is when he wrote :

> Neither a borrower nor a lender be
> For the loan often loseth both itself and the friend
> And borrowing dulls the edge of husbandry.

We pride ourselves that we do not owe anybody anything. Are you sure ?

Our Debt to the Past

We were born into a ready-made world. It was not all it might be and we have been complaining about its deficiencies and limitations ever since. But it was a great deal better than it used to be. One of my regular journeys takes me up a village street where on one side of the road is a new estate of what are the pet abomination of many people, Council houses. On the other side is a huddled collection of the cottages of a century ago. The contrast is dramatic. Whatever limitations the Council houses have, compare them with the workmen's houses across the street and be thankful. To-day we are trying to raise the school-leaving age to fifteen. A century ago children of five worked eighteen hours a day, and in many towns more than half the total population was receiving poor relief.

Improvements did not come about by chance or luck or by some law of inevitable progress ; men and women fought and suffered and struggled and died to make the world a better place for their children. Have you paid your debt to them ? Have you measured the sacrifice and love of the people who built your chapel? We complain at the cost of keeping it up, but they built it. What of the debt you owe to your home ? Count the sacrifices those who loved you made for you that you might have a better start in life than they had had. Measure all the patience, hope and faith with which they cared for you. Calculate the worth of your inheritance of a good character which made it difficult, and almost impossible, for you to do any other than go straight. A good physical constitution is a great thing, but what is a good moral constitution worth ? Have you paid that debt ? Is there any way in which you can pay it but by striving to leave the world better than you found it ?

Our Debt to the Present

All the good men are not dead and all the good is not in the past. How much do we owe to the good people of our own time ? Suppose all the Sunday motorists went on strike and all the Sunday hikers stayed at home ; would anybody be a penny the worse ? Would there be any less kindness or friendship, sympathy or love in the world ? But suppose that all the Sunday-school teachers and local preachers struck. Suppose all the people who run hospitals and visit workhouses and serve in welfare clinics, and run Scouts and Guides and do all manner of service for other people, asking for no reward, were to throw up their jobs ; what would happen ? What a debt we owe to them all.

What a debt we owe for the common things of everyday life ! Do you remember the old Scots song ; ' Caller Herrin ! ' ' Wives and mithers, maist despairin ',' call it ' lives o' men.' Have you paid your debt to the men who go down to the sea in ships and to the women who love them, when you have paid the fishmonger ? Now and then the world is shocked by some mining disaster, but we never think of the loss of life which goes on every day and the price the collier's wife pays for coal. Have you paid your debt when you paid the coal merchant ? Have you paid your debt to the men who died in the war to end war when you subscribed to the War Memorial ?

How much do you owe to the friends you have ; the people who have stood by us and befriended us in times when we did not deserve it and had no claim upon their friendship and love. When Paul wrote to his friend, Philemon, asking him to take back and forgive the runaway slave, Onesimus, Paul said, ' If he owes you anything put it down to my account. Here is my I.O.U., my own signature. But remember, that you owe me, over and above that, your very soul ' (Philemon 18-19). Is there not someone who can say the same thing to you ? If there is, pass it on. Service for others is the only way in which we can pay the debt we owe to those who have served us. ' Service is the rent we pay for our room on earth.'

Our Debt to God

How much owest thou to thy Lord ? We may not have all we wish but how much we have still. Do you thank God that you can see, and hear and walk, that He has kept your mind clear, that you have work to do and strength to do it ? Do you thank Him for the way you look at life, that you can see the best and make the best of things, for that also is His gift ? How much do you owe for the privilege of taking everything to God in prayer, for that something decent within you which will not let you stray ? How much do you owe for sins forgiven, for sorrows comforted, for strength for weary days ?

> O to grace how great a debtor,
> Daily I'm constrained to be.

XIV

SAY IT WITH FLOWERS

WHAT a wonderful place the modern florist's window is with his delightful invitation, ' Say it with Flowers.' He fills it with flowers the whole year round. Before chrysanthemums are ended his window is ablaze with the golden glory of daffodils. He deserves everyone's praise and thanks for the way he makes the world a brighter, cheerier place. He is always giving us new varieties and colours of sweet peas and violas, roses and carnations. Not that it is all gain. There was something to be said for the old cottage window filled with geraniums in ochre-painted pots. And some of us would sacrifice a good deal of form and colour for the profusion and fragrance of the old cabbage roses. But the florist's slogan has become a motto of every-day life.

How did you say it ?

' I would take anything from her. She has such a nice way of saying things.' Have you earned that compliment ? You have listened to a preacher and have come away refreshed and renewed. ' What did he say ? ' someone asks. ' I don't know,' you reply, ' but I know he did me good.' It was not what he said but the way he said it. There are some preachers who give you splendid stuff but their manner says, ' I hope you are interested. I'm not, very much,' and you almost expect to see him stop and yawn in the middle of his own sermon.

How did you say it ? Some people say it with

flowers ; some with brickbats. They are sarcastic, bitter, contemptuous. How they rejoice in a direct hit—' That caught you on the raw,' they chuckle, ' that dusted your feathers for you. And, remember, I haven't said half the nasty things I think about you.' ' Neither have I,' you retort, and one bitter word fetches another. You fight with poisoned arrows and even after the arrow has been pulled out, the poison is still in your blood.

Someone says that friends and acquaintances can be classified as plus and minus people. The plus people add something to you. They give you courage and cheer. You feel that you are better and that the world is a pleasanter place because you have met them. They say it with flowers. The minus people subtract something from you. They depress and trouble you, take from you light and joy, hope and peace. They never bring you flowers.

Say it nicely

If a thing is to be done, do it pleasantly ; that is what the florists' motto says. Flowers are always appropriate, or nearly always. There is a story of a very sick man who, when his friend asked him whether he should send fruit or flowers, replied, gloomily, ' It is too late for fruit and a little too early for flowers.' But such people are happily rare. A pleasant word is never out of place, and a nice thing, nicely said, is always welcome. We may not live for praise, but we live better if we get it. We are all cheered and helped by appreciation.

The cynic says : ' What's the good of flowers ? They only fade.' That is true, but the memory of them does not fade, and their fragrance lives and abides.

And the memory of the kindly, appreciative word lives on long after the echo has died away in silence. How much attention people are paying now to wrappers. Things are being nicely put up and attractively packed. Wrapping paper is grey, or green, or lavender, and the parcel is a little more welcome, somehow. It is not done for fun, it is saying it with flowers. Food may not be better eaten from a tablecloth than from a newspaper, but it tastes better and, as a matter of fact, it is better.

I saw a menu recently of a Foreign Affairs Banquet, which was just a Foreign Missionary Supper in evening dress. You could not have a collection at a banquet, equally you could not have a banquet without tips, so there was a note : ' The waitresses have kindly consented to give their tips to the cause of Foreign Missions.' That was saying it with flowers, surely. What a difference there is between the person who, when asked to do something, makes endless excuses : ' I don't think I can. I don't like that sort of thing. Is there nobody else ? ' and eventually says, ' I suppose I must ' ; and that other person who smiles and says : ' It will be a privilege to do it.' What a difference the flowers make ! Who get most work done ; the mistress who is always nagging and grumbling ; or the mistress who strokes you the right way ?

No Flowers, by request

The people for whom they are intended will not be there to see them, so why keep flowers for funerals ? Do you know the story of Thomas Carlyle mourning his dead wife and crying : ' If only I could tell her how I loved her.' But he had always been too busy to think of buying flowers and now funeral flowers were too late.

How disheartening it is to work hard all day for someone who never notices. You felt pleased and proud with the look of the house but Jim never noticed. If only he had said, ' It looks nice,' how much it would have meant. If only you had told Jim that, in spite of all his faults, you would not change him for any other husband in the street it would have been worth while. Jim praises the things his mother used to cook, but you wonder if he ever told her so while he lived at home. Some people are spoiled by praise but far more people are spoiled for the lack of it.

So be generous with your flowers ; the more freely they are picked the more freely they will bloom. If they are not picked they will go to seed and cease to blossom. Whatever has to be said or done, say it with flowers ; it is easier for you and nicer for others.

XV

POSTMAN'S KNOCK

You need not blush. This has nothing to do with the games they were playing at the Junior Guild Party last Wednesday, but with the double knock which comes more or less regularly at your door when ' Postie ' comes up the street. We seldom remember to give thanks for these common things which make so much difference in our lives. In many modern Sunday Schools the leader teaches the children to pray by asking them to suggest for what things they shall ask God and for what blessings give Him thanks. A leader in an East

London school when asking for suggestions for thanksgiving received the unusual suggestion, ' Please, miss, fag-cards.' And when you remember how much joy and interest cigarette cards brought into the narrow poverty-stricken life of the child you thank God for the child's sincerity.

Do you ever thank God for Rowland Hill and the penny post ? It is now nearly one hundred years old. Before that, to send a letter from London to Edinburgh cost 1/-, cash on delivery. Many a poor woman could not afford the postage on the letter some loved one had sent her from overseas ; it might cost half a week's wage—now, if the postman passes us by we say, ' No news is good news.' We know that those we love will not be debarred from writing to us because they cannot afford the postage and that we shall not be cut off from them because we cannot afford to receive it. Thanks be to God for a cheap and rapid postal system.

Postman's Knock

How many times eager, anxious eyes watch the postman come up the street ! He is coming nearer, he is crossing the road, and he goes next door. You go back to your work but you have no heart in it. But if you hear the click of your letter-box and the rat-tat of your knocker, you dry your hands on your apron and hurry up the passage. As likely as not it is only the gas-bill or an advertisement of a sale of fur coats, and you are disappointed again. But more often you pick it up eagerly, one glance at the writing is sufficient, and you settle down to read the news ; Fanny was always such a good letter writer, and somehow, when you start work again, you feel as fresh as though you had only just begun.

As the Bible puts it in a lovely picture : ' As cold waters to a thirsty soul, so is good news from a far country ' (Proverbs xxv. 25).

Some letters are different. A single look at the envelope and you sigh, ' I wonder what is the matter now ? ' Henrietta always seems to have had all the trouble in the world, and then some more added to it.

' Post time is adventure time,' says a familiar advertisement, and it is perfectly true. You never know what the postman will bring. Do you remember those war years when your heart almost stopped for fear every time you heard that double knock at your door ?

> Just a tiny message,
>   In a yellow envelope,
> Came an end of all things—
>   Even hope.

What wonderful letters the postman brings sometimes from people who have learned to use what Dr. J. R. Miller used to call ' A golden pen'! It was only a steel nib usually, but the words and the message were more golden than gold. Walt Whitman, an American poet, said, ' I find letters from God dropped in the street.' Do you know what he meant ? ' In the beginning was the Word . . . the Word became flesh and dwelt among us ' (John i. 1, 14). A letter from God. So was Paul and Wesley and many a good soul you have known, letters in which God told His love and kindness and mercy.

Not Afraid

Do you know where the postman's knock is mentioned in the Bible ? Look up Psalm cxii. 7. Read the whole

Psalm and see the picture of the man who was not afraid to open his letters in the morning. See the secret of his fearlessness. ' His heart is fixed, trusting in the Lord.' ' Thou wilt keep him in perfect peace whose mind is stayed on Thee ' (Isa. xxvi. 3). He shall not be afraid of the postman's knock. Even if the postman brings bad news :

> Ill that He blesses is our good,
>   And unblest good is ill,
> And all is right that seems most wrong,
>   If it be His sweet will.

There is a story of an old Puritan preacher who lived in perilous days when no man knew what an hour or a day would bring forth, that when he saw the postman cross the bridge to come to him he would fall upon his knees to claim strength from God for whatever might be coming. Let us thank God that we are not called upon to live in such a day as that. But the woman who has strengthened herself in God will know the difference between ' taking it lying down,' and ' standing up to it,' if ill news should come.

There is a delightful story in the Bible of a king to whom the postman brought ill news. It was an insulting letter, a letter which was like a basket of scorpions, every word was poisonous, every sentence had a sting in its tail. It was a threatening letter. It threatened all manner of ill and disaster, and the king knew that the man who wrote the letter was not uttering empty threats. He was able to do all he threatened to do, and more. ' And Hezekiah went up to the house of the Lord and spread the letter before the Lord ' (Isa. xxxvii. 14). And the Lord sent a peaceful answer down. If you get letters that frighten and hurt,

ollow Hezekiah's example and the Lord will see and
answer. You need not be afraid of the postman's
knock.

XVI

FEBRUARY FILL-DYKE

FEBRUARY is the most dreary and miserable month
of the whole year,' Mrs. Grump complains. ' You
have nothing but grey skies overhead and mud under-
foot and everyone you meet is under the weather,
and no wonder.' Mrs. Grump is not alone in her opinion.
No poet, as far as I know, ever wrote a poem in praise
of February, they kept their praises for the Spring and
the Autumn. No proud mother ever called her daughter
February, though many have called their children June,
and April. But ' February Fill-dyke ' would sound too
much like a prophecy of lamentation.

But there is much to be said for February. If we
had no February we should have no roses in June and
no corn in September. That was one of the lessons
we learned unwillingly during the long droughts of the
past two years and each year wise men carefully watch
the rainfall to see what the prospects are for full dykes
in each dreary, unwelcome, February month. Some
people have suggested that the real reason why the
month was shortened was that we could endure no more
of it. It is far more true to say that we could not do
with less of it.

Raining Daffodils

I like the faith and the spirit of the poet who looked

E

out of his window on a dreary, dripping, February d
and sang,

> And on the distant hills
> It isn't raining rain to me,
> It's raining daffodils.

For that is a charmingly beautiful and wholly tr
little parable of life. Who, unless they had seen it a
proved it would have believed that the grey skies
February would be transformed into the gold
daffodils of April and the fruitful fields of Autumn ?

But is not that always the way of our Heaver
Father, not only in the world of Nature, but in th
more precious world of the spirit when He sows bet
seed and reaps harvests unto life everlasting ? There
another favourite verse of mine which expresses
perfectly :

> The rain that fell a-yesterday is ruby on the roses,
>   Silver on the poplar-leaf and gold on the willow-stem ;
> The grief that chanced a-yesterday is silver that encloses
>   Holy loves where time and change shall never trouble
>   them.

We would blot out the days of February from t
calendar if we could have our way. As soon as Chri
mas is past Spring would arrive overnight, but if we h
our way what a tragedy the year would be and h
quickly we should be praying that God would ord
our years and our weather according to His wisdom a
not according to our folly. It is from the full dykes
February that we drink and renew our strength
the delightful sun-filled days of June and wash oursel
from the dust and stickiness which are insepara
from fine weather and sunny days. Summer, even
it kept its beauty, would be unbearable were it not f
what the deep springs and the subsoil store up

February.   April showers refresh the face of the earth
but the heavy rains of February fill the deep springs.
Is not that one of the ways in which our Heavenly
Father says to us ' My ways are not your ways . . .
but as the heavens are high above the earth so are My
ways higher than your ways ' ? (Isa. lv. 9).

If we could have our way, for ourselves and for those
we love most and best, all our days would be Summer,
life would be one long June, but how foolish it would all
be. We shall need all the February rains before the year
is through.   We still need our share of sorrow and our
days of tears before life is through.   Remember the
tragedy of Moab, whose year had had no February.
(Jer. xlviii. 11.)   If we had no rainy days we could
never make hay when the sun shines, as a proverb says.

It is as true of our service as of our characters.
Thomas Fuller, an old Puritan preacher, says that one
day on his rounds he saw a man working in the fields.
It was a day of pouring rain and the very roads were
quagmires.   Fuller sympathized with the man for
having to work in the open on such a day.   The man
answered with a laugh that it was a perfect day for his
task,   ' Sow beans in the mud, they'll come up like a
wud ' (wood).   There was a Psalmist who knew it too.
(Psalm cxxvi. 5-6.)

So let us thank God for February days, in spite of all
the Mrs. Grumps of this world.   Is not this the message
of our Heavenly Father for every February day in the
calendar and in life : ' Who passing through the valley
of weeping make it a well ; the rain also filleth the
pools ' ? (Psalm lxxxiv.6). From those pools men shall
drink and lift up their heads.   (Psalm cx. 7.)

XVII

MARCH WINDS

WHEN I met Mrs. Grump the other afternoon an ventured to remark that we were getting through th Winter very nicely, she shook a gloomy head an remarked emphatically, ' But we have March to g through yet.' Of course, that is perfectly true and good many people with weak chests and a tendency rheumatism will be more than a little relieved whe March is past.

Still, Mrs. Grump's remark depressed me a t and she saw it and said, ' But, then, as the Goe Book says, " God tempers the wind to the sho lamb," so I suppose He will help us to get throug March.'

I felt that it was not worth while to tell the de soul that the proverb she quoted is not in the Bib Most people think it is just as they believe that escape by the skin of one's teeth is a quotation fro Shakespeare. (See Job xix. 20.) There is somethi very like it in the Bible, though, which is a very go word with which to face our battle with March wine ' He stayed His rough wind in the day of the east wine (Isa. xxvii. 8).

The Revised Version changes it considerably, but am quite sure that the word is true, whatever t prophet may actually have written. And Mrs. Grum version was good gospel even if it was never in t Bible ; because it has been true to the experience the children of God in all generations.

The Big Bad Wolf

Now will all you people who are afraid of the big bad wolf who howls and tears and rages in the winds of March and threatens to bring your house of health and home and happiness about your ears lay hold upon his word—' His rough wind ' ? Have you remembered that the winds are His, even the rough wind ? We thought that the winds were something altogether beyond His control, we feared that the most He could do for us was to protect us from the worst of their fury, to be ' a shelter in the time of storm.' But if the rough wind is His wind, that changes things. There was a Psalmist who had caught a glimpse of the truth, and when he called upon all things in earth, and air, and sea to praise the great Creator he included, ' stormy wind fulfilling His word ' (Psalm cxlviii. 8).

We could not have a good year of harvest without the storm winds of March. ' March dust is worth a guinea a bushel,' my farmer friends used to tell me as the storms swept across the bare fields and whipped the branches of the leafless trees. That was what the winds were doing. And, though I am not wise enough yet to understand it, March winds have their place in the scheme of life. For telegraph poles which must stand in exposed places and bear the weight and strain of many wires they commonly use pine tree trunks. But the pine tree gathers its strength from its battles with the March winds and the twisting and straining of the fibres mean that it ' comes more than conqueror,' as St. Paul would put it. The tree not only triumphs in its battle with the storm but is actually made by the battle. You cannot grow strong, tough wood in glass-houses or even in sheltered valleys, but in places where the March winds blow.

> Whichever way the wind may blow
> Some heart is glad to have it so,

I saw on one of those poker-work mottoes in a shop window the other day. It set me thinking. My little vessel is not the only ship on the sea, and though the wind may hinder me there will be many another little ship which that hindering wind will be blowing towards the harbour where it will be safe. It may make my chimney smoke but it will make someone else's chimney draw well. I am not the only child in my Father's house and He has to think of His other children as well as think of me. But He has such love for me that He will never allow me to suffer. He was a wise old saint who said, ' When I think of all my Father has to do I cannot see how He can have time to remember me, yet when I think of all that He does for me I cannot think that He has anyone else to care for.'

Measuring the Strain

So I know that the rough wind and the east wind will never blow together, and I am grateful for that. I remember going over a great steel works where iron pipes were being cast, and the engineer in charge, as he showed us the spinning moulds into which the molten metal was run, told us that the water which was poured on the moulds was to keep them at a special temperature and that it was exerted at a special pressure and afterwards the pipes were passed through a furnace in which they were hardened at a carefully regulated speed. Any variation in the pressure of the water on the moulds or in the time taken by the pipes to pass through the hardening process would be disastrous. If an engineer can regulate as wisely and carefully as that the strain which an iron pipe can stand, my Heavenly Father will not be less wise or less careful in measuring the strain for the making of character in His children. ' He will stay His rough wind in the day of the east wind.'

The Bible is never contradicted by experience. And has not this been your experience? You have been tested and strained but you have never been allowed to reach the breaking point. ' I should never have believed it if I had not gone through it.' Of course not. All the best things of God are so wonderful that we should have said they were too good to be true if we had not experienced them. That is why if March comes in like a lion it goes out like a lamb. The winds threaten to uproot us but they leave us more deeply-rooted than ever, more secure and strong. They are His winds and He will see that they are not more than we can bear. And, afterwards, when the March winds have blown themselves out, Spring will be here, new leaves on the trees, and flowers in the hedges. The year needs its March winds but the year is not all March. ' Lord we thank Thee that it is not always like this,' prayed Dr. Stalker one slushy, stormy winter morning, as he opened the service. And even when it is ' A Man shall be a hiding-place from the wind and a covert from the tempest ' (Isaiah xxxii. 2), even when the ' blast of the terrible ones is as a storm against the wall ' (Isaiah xxv. 4)

> The Lord's our Rock, in Him we hide,
> A shelter in the time of storm.

XVIII

KEEPING LENT

ALL good wives and mothers will have been reminded of the beginning of Lent by the coming of Pancake Day, one of the few old Lenten customs which survive. Originally the Pancake Bell, which they still ring in some parishes on the morning of Shrove Tuesday, called people to come to church for confession at the beginning of Lent. Later it became the signal for the commencement of all manner of festivities, including, of course, the eating of pancakes. It is curious what a gift man has for making customs meet his own desires.

Not many people keep Lent in these days, in the old sense of the word and, frankly, I do not see any reason why they should do so. What self-denial there is in eating fish on Fridays instead of meat and feasting on salmon instead of steak I have never been able to understand. If it was a real self-denial and self-sacrifice there would be much to be said for it. Robert Herrick, an old Elizabethan poet, says the wisest word I know on the subject ;

> It is to fast from strife,
>   From old debate and hate ;
> To circumcise thy life.
>   To show a heart grief-rent
> To starve thy sin, not Bin,
>   And that's to keep thy Lent.

For so many people Lent is not a voluntary observance but a compulsory one in these days, and the season lasts the whole year round. There is no need to preach economy and self-denial to those whose lives know little else, who must look both sides of a penny and make it do the work of two. What room is there for keeping Lent or what call to observe it ?

Letting Ourselves Go

Yet it is a good thing to keep Lent if only to fight against the ever present temptation to let ourselves go. There is always a peril of growing slack and careless. An Education Authority was reporting the other day that one result of the films has been to make girls ' clothes-conscious.' Everyone knows how true that is. Yet how many of the girls who make such efforts to look smart and attractive when they go to the office or the mill seem to lose all that ' clothes-consciousness ' after they are married. It is so easy to grow slovenly and untidy when you are alone all day and there is no one to dress for. Of course, John will be coming home, but then he is only John and he does not matter.

Then there is a call to pull ourselves together. John's sister is coming to stay, or we move into a nicer neighbourhood. Now we have to be a little more particular how we look in the mornings ; we look for something new and smart in overalls, the house gets an extra clean. It may even run to a little extra attention to hair and hands. Even John notices it and shows his appreciation in very pleasant ways. After all, that pull up was worth while. The call to keep Lent is an opportunity to do something of the same sort for our souls, our characters ; to do a little spiritual spring cleaning.

Keep Lent with God

It is so easy to grow slack in the things of the deeper

life and so hard to pull up. How hard it is to make time to pray in the morning. If you try to snatch a few minutes after breakfast is over and the children are gone to school you cannot forget the table waiting to be cleared and the fireplace waiting to be cleaned. You make up your mind that, whatever happens, you will sit down and listen to the Daily Service on the Wireless at 10-15. But all the time you are fidgeting about the floors and the washing-up and the shopping and the dinner. And at night you are too tired to pray.

Why not keep Lent ? Make up your mind that in spite of the littered table and the shopping you will enter into your inner chamber and shut your door and pray to your Father which is in secret, and your Father which seeth in secret will reward you openly. Make up your mind to try it during Lent. You will not be behind with your work when dinner-time comes round. And if you make a habit of it until Easter you will have got into the way of it and the rest will be easy.

Keep Lent with Others

If you have any idea that God has any pleasure in the conventional keeping of Lent which ends with the banning of pictures and chocolates—though to do as much as that for Lent might be a good thing—read Isaiah lviii—'Is not this the fast that I have chosen ? ' Keep a better Lent than that. Why not deny ourselves unkind and unpleasant gossip ? Gossip is human and may be a great blessing. But let us have no unkind gossip during Lent, let us keep it to ourselves and only repeat and pass on the happy and the pleasant things. ' I heard such a lovely thing said about you the other day.' Pass on that bit of gossip ; it is much too good to keep. 'What do you think Priscilla Perkins did last week?' Repeat the story of her kindness and devotion and thoughtfulness for old Mrs. Grump.

And keep a Lent of bad tempers; even on the things which are your pet annoyances. Perhaps it is an untidy room and husbands are such untidy creatures, they throw things down anywhere. And some of us get annoyed if we are kept waiting, we hate wasting time. Possibly it is an unpleasant habit of someone else's which always gets on our nerves and makes us irritable and cross; or it may be that we grow impatient with the denseness and ignorance of those with whom we have to do. Let us keep Lent with God and with others. Is not this the fast which He has chosen? And let us thank Him for the call to pull ourselves together.

XIX

VALENTINES

No ONE knows who St. Valentine was or what happened to him. There have been many saints who bore the name of Valentine and which is commemorated on February 14 no one seems to know. But the Early Church seldom attempted to change old customs in the life of the people. They kept the custom and changed the idea. There was an old belief that on this day the birds chose their mates, so the Church dedicated the day to St. Valentine and made him the patron saint of all true lovers. Games were played in which every Jack had his Jill and every Jill her Jack. If Jack did not want that particular Jill he sent her a present instead. A generation or two ago when St. Valentine enjoyed a greater popularity hundreds of thousands of Valentines were delivered by burdened postmen. Then the habit degenerated into vulgarity and attempts to revive it have not been very successful.

What Was Behind It ?

Behind every old custom, however foolish it seems, there was something deep and real. The Victorian miss, watching from behind the curtains for the postman on Valentine's Day, was watching for something more than the postman. She was wondering what life would bring. She was convinced that life had not only been planned wisely for her, like some problem in mathematics, but that life had been planned lovingly, without grudging or restraint—

> Givest me all I ask and more,
> Makes my cup of joy run o'er.

I suppose one could get through life without love and affection, but what a poor thing life would be. We feel that we were planned for something fairer and greater than that, that to be loved, cared for, fussed over, is part of God's will and purpose for us. I read of a man whose constant song was,

> ' I'm glad of my daily bread,
>   And that's more than can be expected,'
> And that was all he said.

I would rather be the girl who waited for her Valentine, even if she waited in vain. I would rather believe that life was intended to be rich with joy and love and a sense of being wanted by someone and precious to someone. It is better to believe in a love that never came than not to believe in love at all.

Love that was Faithful

The real value of the Valentine was what it did for you. It means so much if we feel that someone believes in us, looks up to us, feels that we are very precious ; it separates us from the crowd. Many a girl whom no one noticed because she was so plain and ordinary suddenly becomes beautiful when she is loved. It is not the result of careful make-up but of something that shines out from within and makes all the difference. Assuredly it was true love which sent the Valentine. That was what made it so precious. Do you remember the sort of verses which were printed on them. They were like this—

> This little tribute which I send,
>   I hope you will receive ;
> And keep it for the sake of one,
>   Who never will deceive.

You have had that feeling when you have watched a wedding and have heard people take great, solemn vows, ' For better for worse ; for richer for poorer ; in sickness and in health.' Few people were thinking about that. They were studying the bride's dress and listening to the nervousness in the bridegroom's voice and wondering whether the best man would drop the ring. If you had stopped to tell them of your fears and to ask them if they were sure they would have laughed at you.

Their love was Valentine love, faithful and true. It would not be with them as it had been with others. Their love would stand the strain, the wear and tear of life, would last. And this is so often true. Vows are kept and then you keep out of the newspapers. If things were worse instead of better they made the best of it ;   if sickness came, they carried the burden courageously and cheerfully ; met disappointment with hope and kept on.

Love that was Generous

Valentines are often more than a lace-edged card.   A diamond ring or a jewelled pendant would be hidden in them ; or perhaps a ribbon or a handkerchief that was more valuable than the jewels because of the love behind it.   Love is like that.   Love loves to give and give and longs to give still more, and does not talk of its sacrifice but of its privilege.   And the love of God is like that, love that is personal, faithful, generous.   If I, a weak, sinful man think about you like that ; love to give you all the best and make life rich and full for you ; if I want to give you a smile for your sadness ; courage for your despair, strength for your weakness, how much more does your Heavenly Father ?   He is the patron saint of all true lovers, eager to give them the best of all true love that our souls may be filled. His is Valentine love, a love that never will deceive.

XX

GATHERING VIOLETS

THERE is something very beautiful about the sayings of the English countryside.   Country people have time to think ; it takes townsfolk all their time to dodge the traffic.   And in their long days of lonely labour, men and women have often been able to think out the meaning of life, and sum up the accumulated experience of many generations in a phrase or a sentence as fresh as an April morning, and as full of life as a field of springing corn. Do you know anything more beautiful than the old proverb about Mothering Sunday. ' He who goes a-mothering finds violets in the lane.' You can smell the scent of the violets in the very words ; and the picture they call up is as beautiful as the thought. It is not at all the sort of thing you could have thought out whilst you leaned against a Belisha beacon and watched the cars race by.

Mothering Sunday began, so the authorities say, because the Epistle for the Fourth Sunday in Lent, Gal. iv. 26. contains the words, ' Jerusalem which is above is free, which is the mother of us all.' That was made an excuse for processional visits to the mother church of the diocese or of the parish and, by a natural process, later in the day, people visited their own mothers bearing specially made cakes and seeking once more a mother's blessing. Now there is, especially in America, a widespread movement to revive the day, and men are urged to attend church wearing a white flower in honour of their mothers.

In Praise of Mothers

I have written more than a score of books, but among the many books I hope to find time to write some day is a book on the Mothers of the Bible. They were not all wise and good mothers. But to-day let us remember those whom we can praise with all our hearts. Have you ever tried to think how much Samuel owed to Hannah ?

There is many a dark and terrible hint of the moral atmosphere of the Tabernacle at Shiloh in which he spent all his early years. What kept him pure and clean, the kind of lad who could hear the voice of God when it called him, but the influence of his mother? It was so much more than a new coat which she brought him when she came to him twice a year. And when he grew older, old enough to understand, it would be an easy thing for him to slip home across the hills to talk things over with his mother. What would he be more likely to do than that?

And Timothy, Paul says, owes his faith to his mother and his grandmother. (2 Tim. i. 5.) And you can only measure the value of that statement when you remember that he had a Greek father and that he grew up in a heathen, degraded town—the town of Lystra, where Paul was stoned and left for dead. So you can go on to tell of what the Lord Jesus owed to His mother, Mary. She kept all the things the angels said and pondered them in her heart, and they must have coloured every word she spoke to her Son and all her thoughts about Him and all her dealings with Him. He was only able to endure all the strain and labour of the years of His ministry because He had had a good mother.

Methodism is the child of John Wesley, but how much it owes to his mother! You only have to recall the way she trained her children to see her influence coming out at every turn and the counsel she gave her headstrong son in critical hours, especially in the matter of local preachers, has been the making of Methodism. America worships Abraham Lincoln as her patron saint, but Lincoln says of the mother who, though she died when he was only nine years of age, had taught him to read and write and inspired him with her own love of learning, ' All that I am and all that I hope to be, I owe to my angel mother. Blessings on her memory!'

Scented Violets

Among certain sections of young people homes are
not greatly valued now-a-days, except as places to eat,
drink, and sleep in and, above all, to dress in ; and
mothers are looked on as a sort of superior general
servant whose main business is to get meals, iron dresses
and press trousers. You know that familiar story of
the boy who had just started work and boasted of the
hours he and his father worked and the wages they
earned. His friend asked him of the hours mother
worked and the amount of work she did and then
asked concerning her wages. ' Wages,' the boy cried
in amazement, ' Mother gets no wages ; she never
does any work ! '

It is a great thing to take mother home the wages of
love and gratitude. You will always find, like the
people who carried home a Simnel cake on Mothering
Sunday, that you have won a mother's blessing, you
will find it literally, splendidly true, that violets will
blossom along the road you walk. You will be cheered
with their promise of spring and the air you breathe
will be scented with their fragrance. The tragedy
comes when we leave it until it is too late and the only
violets we can find are those whose perfume is lost in
the heavy scent of funeral flowers. Keep Mothering
Sunday this year.

F

XXI

APRIL FOOLS

IF YOU have children in the house or children in the street there will be little or no hope of forgetting the fact that the first of April is All Fools' Day. All manner of ancient jokes will be revived and old tricks will be played on the unwary and the unsuspecting. I feel sometimes that I should like to make a great religious festival of it and keep the Feast of All Splendid Fools. I should like to devise a great pageant, all full of bright colour and wonderful music, and make a parade of all the men whom once the world called fools, with whom now the rich and wise would be ready to change places.

I would have a section of that pageant for men who refused to be millionaires ; men like Sir Humphrey Davy who, when he invented the miner's safety lamp, refused to patent it lest mine owners should say that it was too dear for them to supply it to their men. Sir Ronald Ross would be there, he who discovered the secret of the scourge of yellow fever and saved scores of thousands of lives and yet was so poor that he had to sell his papers to buy bread and butter. What an army of missionaries would march in that procession, with David Livingstone at their head, men who counted not their lives dear unto them for their brethrens' sake. Wesley would ride upon his horse, and Robert Raikes, whom the men of Gloucester called 'Bobby Wildgoose,' would lead his Sunday-school children, men like Barnardo and Stephenson would be there ; the good Earl Shaftesbury and William Wilberforce, all men whom the world called fools.

And the Women

And the women would mostly be women of whom the world has never heard, of whom the world was not worthy. Elizabeth Fry, in her plain Quaker dress, might lead them, for she was a fool to leave her quiet home in Norfolk to care for the women in Newgate who were so violent that the Governor dared not visit without a guard. Florence Nightingale with her lamp would walk beside her, for she was a fool to make herself such a nuisance to the British War Office that they had to send her to the Crimea to be rid of her. But for the most part they would be women who declined offers of marriage and homes and children of their own because they felt they had a duty to care for someone else who needed them, and grew faded and old and were at last unwanted.

That procession would include the women who gave their love to worthless husbands and only gave them greater love when they proved less worthy of it ; all the women who spent themselves caring for children who did not deserve it and who, because they did not deserve it, could not appreciate it ; all the people of whom others said, ' Why is she fool enough to put up with it ? ' I see all the mothers in their shabby clothes who went without that the children might look nice ; all who wore themselves out with labour that the children might have leisure and a good time ; and, as they marched, there would be a light upon their faces like the light of those who face the sun. I know, because I have seen it.

Whose Fool are You ?

There would be a section for local preachers and Sunday-school teachers, choir members and guide mistresses, all who spend their Sundays serving others instead of going hiking or motoring, and they would march to the music in their souls ; for they are the people who have music. It is one of the strange laws of life that the more you give the more you have. It is as true of love and happiness as it is true of time and money. The wealth and abundance of these things by which men live is not won by searching for it but by spending it. The things for which no one thanks you ; the service for which others call you a fool, are the things by which we live. The unshared bread is taste-less and stale and the unshared water is flat and dull. When we are fools enough to share it we find how sweet it may be.

I have known a good many splendid fools ; mostly men whom others described as fools to themselves. A friend of mine who is a Salvation Army officer some-times parades the streets wearing an embroidered jersey, which has on the front the words, ' A fool for Christ's sake,' and on the back, ' Whose fool are you ? ' The Lord Jesus knew a fool who was not very splendid, the rich fool. Singularly, he was the man of whom everybody said, ' He's no fool.' His bursting barns and his growing bank balance were proof of that. He was like an American millionaire who died a while ago of whom a newspaper remarked bitterly : ' The loss is fully covered by the insurance.' What a fool he had been to hoard his money, a fool to himself ! The laughter of little children whom he had helped and healed would have cheered him and he had missed it. The blessings of those whose burdens he had lifted would have enriched him and he robbed himself of it. His money might have gone on blessing the world after he had gone, but he forgot it. He saved his money, and lost all his money might have meant. What a fool he was! ' He that loveth his life shall lose it,' it sounds the greatest folly, but it is the most splendid truth. I am glad there is an All Fools' Day in the calendar of the year.

XXII

THIS SPRING BUSINESS

MAY I remind you that according to the Calendar, March 21 is the first day of Spring, so now you know whether you are correct in saying, ' What an early Spring we are having,' or ' How late the Spring is this year.' Mrs. Grump and her friends say that this Spring business is very much overdone and that there is no sense in all the fuss we make about it. It is a most uncomfortable time of the year. It is too mild for Winter clothes and too cool for Summer things. You can never tell what to do. If it is June in the morning it is November at night. You set off hoping for a sunbath and you come home drenched with fog.

The drapers and the tailors try to make a fuss about it. ' Your old frock looks shabby in the Spring sunshine,' they say, and you know that well enough. ' Look at your hat,' they shout at you ; and you have been looking at it until you are tired of the sight of it. But you think you can manage with it a bit longer. It will do as long as this uncertain weather lasts. Then you think again. No, it won't. Anything was good enough for the mackintosh and umbrella weather of a few weeks ago but you really do feel shabby now in that dull coat and that hat is an absolute wreck. And that is the way the money goes.

Spring-cleaning is the next item on the programme. The one word on every woman's tongue is, ' I never saw the place look so dirty in my life,' and there is no rest until you have been through the house from top to bottom. People rave about the smell of Spring flowers, but Spring means the smell of soft soap and half-dry paint ; poets write about the glories of Spring, beautiful Spring, and you suspect they do it between sneezes with their feet in a mustard bath ; soloists sing of the flowers that bloom in the Spring, tra-la ; and apologize for being in poor voice because they are suffering from the usual Spring cold.

The Turn of the Year

When you have recovered from all that it is still true that Spring is the turn of the year. All the sick folk feel they will be better when the Spring comes. ' I shall lose my cough in the Spring and recover my strength ' ; and they do. We do pick up our strength in the sunshine. Think what is done for children even with the artificial sunlight of an electric lamp. Even blind people wither in the dark as a plant does. But now the days are lengthening and things are on the turn. There are catkins on the hazel and furry buds on the willow. There is a touch of green on the lilac buds and the pear blossom is showing white. In a few weeks the hedges will be green and the children will come home with armfuls of bluebells and the apple orchards will be masses of pink. We have all the Summer and Autumn to which to look forward.

We shall be able to do without fires and lamps and that will save a lot of work and worry, scrubbing and dusting ; we shall not have to melt the butter before we can spread it or bother with hot-water bottles at night. Spring means new clothes and more expense. But, never mind that. People will really look nice and the world will look a prettier place when everyone is wearing Spring clothes. And because they look better people will feel fresher. They will not only be nicer to look at, but nicer to speak to and nicer to live with.

Spring cleaning has to be done, but how nice the house will look when it is finished. You have moved the furniture about a bit, changed a chair from by the window to alongside the door, hung a picture over the mantelpiece instead of opposite the window ; you have new, clean curtains up and you almost think you have moved into a new house. Spring is not too bad, after all.

Spring in Your Blood

This Spring business gets into you. Everything catches the Spring fever and renews its youth. Old elms and grey, old apple trees and withered trees that looked dead burst into newness of life. The world is full of young things, chickens and lambs, leafbuds and flowers and we all rejoice in them and renew our youth while we watch them. And that is the will of God for us, that we should renew our youth and that life should be at the Spring. We hail the world where the will of God is done as a place where 'everlasting Spring abides.' This looking forward to brighter days is a movement of the Spirit of God. And He is not deceiving us. It is not an empty dream. His will is that the dream should come true, that the hope should be fulfilled and that the fulfilment should be something greater than all we have ever hoped or imagined.

Spring in your Step

That is what the manufacturer of rubber heels promises me if only I will fit his products to my shoes. He assures me that he will make my way smooth and the journey comfortable ; that he will put Spring into my days. And that also is part of the will of God for me and for all His children. We shall not miss the Winter but we shall come to the Spring. We shall not miss the rough places in the road but we shall get over them. ' Though he fall, he shall not be utterly cast down ' (Psalm xxxvii. 24). He shall walk with a springy step because he has the Springtime of God in his heart. He will find more meanings than one in the old line, ' My God, the spring of all my joys.' Spring, with all its promise of better days, with all its shielding and helping in the journey of life, is God's offer to you. Keep Christ in your heart and you will find that however the year may go and whatever the weather may be ' there,' in your soul, ' everlasting Spring abides.'

XXIII

WOMEN AT THE CROSS

IT IS the Holy Week and the minds of good Christian people in every place will be turning to the story of the Passion of our Lord and will follow Him with reverence and with love who, for us and our redemption became obedient unto death, even the death of the Cross, that we might not perish but have everlasting life. All the days of His earthly life He was ministered to by women. A woman bore Him under her heart and welcomed Him into the world. In the days of His public ministry certain women ministered unto Him of their substance (Luke viii. 2-3), and at the last it was a group of women who stood beneath His Cross (Mark xv. 40-41), and followed Him to His tomb (Mark xv. 47). A long story could be told of all women did for Him in those days, and began a ministry of love and service which has flowed through the years in an ever-widening stream.

His Appeal to Women

Women were of little importance in that day. A good Jew thanked God daily that he had not been born a woman. Woman was either man's slave or his play-thing and, like most other things which man tries to enslave, often enslaved her master. But Jesus raised women to a place of equality and importance with men, and women were quick to see something in His attitude, to detect a tone in His voice which gave their lives a meaning and an importance such as life had not had before. His sympathy for them helped them to sympathize with Him. Surely that was why the women of Jerusalem wept and bewailed Him in an hour when the crowd shouted ' Crucify Him ' (Luke xxiii. 27).

His ministry of help and healing would appeal to women. They knew how greatly women and children suffered and all the deep bitterness of bereavement ; and when He brought back life and health it was their burdens which were lifted ; their sorrows which were comforted. They could not help loving One who had been so kind. Men might criticize His attitude to religious law and argue long about His politics and all that His preaching meant in the conflict with the Roman power. Women were not concerned with such things as these. They loved Him because He had blessed their children and healed their sick.

And His homeliness would appeal to them. They had never known a teacher before who knew anything about baking bread or mending clothes or the price of sparrows in the market. Somehow the homeliness and friendliness of His teaching drew Him near to them. They were sure that they would never again have a Teacher who understood the life of every day as He had done. It was a shameful thing that He should suffer, who had done so much to heal and relieve suffering ; that He should die who could never be replaced. It was no wonder that their lamentations were so loud ; their sorrow so deep.

Women's Loyalty to Him

Men who had protested that they would be loyal to Him, even unto prison and unto death, all forsook Him and fled. The women stood there beneath His Cross, shared His shame, for who can doubt that those who mocked Him mocked also His friends who watched Him ? His suffering must have been almost as terrible for them to watch as it was for Him to bear, but the women stood by, hoping that their very presence would mean comfort and help and strength. Who can measure how much their silent sympathy meant to our Lord in that hour of His desperate need when He felt that even God had forsaken Him ? And who can express the debt of gratitude which the Church in all ages owes to those faithful women ?

It seemed so little ; it meant so much. They were only a group of unimportant women. They could not fight to deliver Him ; they could not plan to go to

Pilate and beg His dear, broken body ; but they could
stand there and watch with Him. Men could not do it
for an hour in a quiet garden, but they did it in the face
of a jeering crowd, through the earthquake and the
terrifying noonday darkness, for all the six hours of
agony and terror and shame. The world expects
women to do things like that. Women have trained
the world to expect them to do it. If a man is faithful
to a worthless wife the world wonders and admires ;
if a woman is true to a worthless husband the world
takes it for granted. It is only what is to be expected.
And in such a day as this when

> Our Lord is now rejected
> And by the world disowned,

it is still the women who remember all they owe to Him,
who do not forget what a Friend they have in Jesus,
who are still found loyal to Him ; who still stand
beneath His Cross. And who can measure what the
women's loyalty means to-day ?

XXIV

WOMEN IN THE EASTER GARDEN

WHAT a perfect thing it is in the Easter story that it
was the women who found that the Lord Jesus had
risen. It was they who had been loyal to Him when
His disciples all forsook Him and fled. They shared
the ' shame and scoffing rude ' which evil men heaped
upon Him ; they were the last at the Cross. What more
fitting than that they should be first at His empty
tomb, the first to share the triumph and the glory of

His resurrection ? One is always glad of the place the women have in the story of Easter Day.

It was scarcely dawn, very early in the morning, the city was still asleep as they passed through it and the dew was still on the grass as they made their way to the garden with the burden of the spices which they had prepared for His dear, dead body. Let all the people who say that the disciples fooled themselves when they said that Jesus had risen from the dead note the evidence of those spices. Suddenly they stopped, you can see the look of dismay on their faces, hear the tremble in their voices, ' who will roll us away the stone ? '

You can enter into that experience because you have passed through it. Someone you loved has passed home to God and sorrow has been like a great stone on your heart. You felt that you never could take up the burden of life again. ' Who will roll away the stone ? ' Or some bitter disappointment had come ; someone on whom you relied had failed you ; Dick's job, that seemed as secure as the Bank of England, had gone ; you faced a future that was all gloomy and dark and without hope. Who will roll away the stone from the place where your hope was buried, and all the ruins of the future were laid ?

' Suppose the women had not gone on ? ' a preacher suggests. But only a man would suggest that. Women always do go on. They may stop and worry ; they may be afraid ; but they go on. And, somehow, the miracle still happens, the stone is rolled away. It is the women who carry on those Churches where the men give up hope ; the women who organize those efforts when men only say, ' whatever are we going to do ? ' The women who find a way to make one shilling do the work of two or three when work fails. And God honours their faith. He sends His angel to roll away the stone—and sit on it. Do not forget that touch in the story. The thing of which you are afraid becomes the seat of the angel of great deliverances.

' Idle Tales '

And when they returned the men said that the story was just an idle tale. ' Hysterical women,' they murmured, ' Poor things ! Their grief has been too much for them. They cannot stand things as men do.' But somehow or other they convinced the men that something had happened, something real and important, and the men had to go and see. ' Man has his will but woman has her way.' It is a good thing for man that she does. Idle tales or not, they made the men go and see for themselves and they not only went, but they ran, ran with all their strength so that John outran Peter and came first to the sepulchre.

Do not get too concerned if people do not believe you the first time ; they may say again that it is just an idle tale when you tell them of something as amazing as the resurrection of the dead. If they do, you will have to convince them, that is all. Argument will do it sometimes, but it will not always succeed, and, somehow, I do not think the women tried to argue that morning. The others saw that something had happened to the women and went to see for themselves. There is a famous story of the way Dr. Dale of Birmingham came to write his famous book, *The Living Christ*. He was writing an Easter sermon, and when half-way through, the thought of the risen Lord broke in upon him as it had never done before. ' " Christ is alive," I said to myself ; alive ! and then I paused ; —alive !

Can that really be true ? Living as really as I myself am ? I got up and walked about repeating, " Christ is living." "Christ is living." It was to me a new discovery . . . I then said, " My people shall know it. I shall preach about it again and again until they believe it as I do now." ' Ever afterwards Dr. Dale began every Sunday morning service with an Easter hymn. ' Idle tales,' but people became convinced.

' Mary ! '

There is one more story in the garden which is far too lovely to be missed. Mary Magdalene, half-blinded with her tears, saw someone whom she thought was a gardener until He spoke to her and called her ' Mary.' That was all. But there was no one in all the world who could say ' Mary,' just as He could. ' He calleth His own sheep by name.' You are not lost in the crowd. Queen Victoria used to complain that Mr. Gladstone spoke to her as though she was a public meeting. Jesus calls us by our name. Will you remember the living Christ this Eastertide, and in the garden and in the kitchen you will hear Someone saying, ' Mary ' ? Someone who knows and understands.

XXV

YOU NEVER CAN TELL

' HALF the interest of life,' says Mrs. Chirp, ' is its unexpectedness. I don't want any one to tell me my fortune, even if they could and I don't believe they can. But if I knew all the good things which were coming

o me there would be no fun in having them come, and
f I knew all the troubles that are coming I should
want to lie down and die at the thought of them.
If Chirp asks me to go to the pictures because he has a
shilling to spare that I didn't know about there's as
much fun in the surprise of being asked as there is in
going. You never know your luck.'

She reminds me of a man of whom I read the other
day. He had a garden in which nothing would grow
except stones and weeds. He planted packets of seeds
and put the pictures on sticks to encourage the seeds
but none came up except those which the cats scratched
up and the birds found. At last, in despair, he sowed a
packet of parrot food and the seeds grew and it was the
greatest joy in the world to see all the queer things
which were growing in that patch. He had more fun
out of it than his neighbour had over his prize dahlias.
It was all so unexpected.

You can never tell how things will turn out. The
dress you made does not look much like the picture on
the cover of the magazine. But the lady in the picture
has a twenty-six inch waistline and yours is only a
memory of the dear, dead days beyond recall and perhaps you did not use quite the best material for that
particular style. Cakes are just the same. You weigh
and measure everything and take special care, and it
turns out to be hard on top and doughy in the middle.
And another time you guess things and make it in a
hurry and it turns out so well that you would not mind
if your mother-in-law, or even Mrs. Grump came to tea.

So you never know how people will turn out. ' I
should never have thought she had it in her,' said Mrs.
Grump the other day when Priscilla Perkins gave the
address, for Priscilla does not belong to one of our *best*

families, and Mrs. G. always says that what's bred in the bone will come out in the flesh, which may be perfectly true, but what *is* bred in the bone ? We should all want to rub out a few names if we could read our family trees, and anyhow, ' There's so much bad in the best of us and so much good in the worst of us, that there's little room for any of us to talk about the rest of us.' But you never can tell.

Can we be Sure ?

Must we say, then, that life is just a kind of Irish Sweep in which you pay your money and chance your luck ? All that is best in us rebels against the idea. We know that life and the world are working to rule all the time. If the cake turned out well it was not a chance happening, but because it really was well mixed and properly baked. The dress would have looked as pretty as the picture if it had been made in the right material and worn by the proper person. You need something more than anxiety and willingness. You need a special sort of hand for gardening, for dressmaking, for cooking and unless you have a light hand with cooking, as Mrs. Chirp has, your pastry will be as ' sad ' and heavy as Mrs. Grump's face, which is not to say that you will not develop that light hand for mixing a cake if you try.

Seeds grow according to their nature. If you sow beetroot you will not get a crop of carrots, and if you sow sweet peas you will not pick dahlias. In spite of all that is unlikely and unexpected you can tell how things will go with you. But not all the results come at the end of the week. God is not like the ' Stores ' who pay ' divi ' once a quarter. But He pays surely and He pays fairly. You have to wait for the big things. You can grow virginia stock or nasturtiums in a week or two, but you have to wait years for an oak or an apple tree to grow. Yet they are worth waiting for.

' Light is sown for the righteous,' said an old Psalmist. (Psalm xcvii. 11.) I know he was old because only an old man who had come to harvest time would have learned it. Mrs. Grump reminds me that ' Curses, like chickens, come home to roost.' Perhaps they do ; but kindness and goodness and love come home to roost, too. You can tell, you can be sure, and if you have to wait the greater will the harvest be. And you can tell about people too. ' I never thought he would turn out like that.' You can always rely on our Heavenly Father. ' with whom is no variableness, neither shadow of turning ' (James i. 17). You can tell that if you put your hand in the fire it will be burned. And you can tell that love will use all its patience, all its wisdom, all its skill to heal the burned hand. The mercy and under-standing of love are as sure as the consequences of sin. Love that heals is as sure as the fire that burns. You can tell that God will never fail.

> Did ever saint find this Friend forsake him ?
> Or sinner find that He would not take Him ?
> No, not one.

When Moses asked for the name of God the reply was ' The God of Abraham, of Isaac and of Jacob ' (Exodus iii. 6), the God of great yesterdays is the God who will be with us in the unknown to-morrow, ' the same yesterday and to-day and for ever ' (Heb. xiii. 8). And Mrs. Chirp cries,' Hallelujah ! You can always tell ! '

G

XXVI

A GOOD 'FORGETORY'

HE was a very wise man who prayed the Lord to bless him with a good forgetory. Half the skill and wisdom of a good memory, under any circumstances, is knowing what to forget. Perhaps the greatest American negro was Booker Washington. He was a cultured gentleman, Principal of a College with over 1,000 students and yet subject to frequent insult on account of his colour. Invited to speak at great functions, when the occasion arrived he would not be called upon because the white people would resent being addressed by a coloured man. But he never grew bitter or resentful. He deliberately cultivated a good forgetory and banished such incidents from his mind. ' I cannot afford to let someone else spoil my life,' he would declare.

The heaviest and most uncomfortable burden any-one can bear is a grudge. It seems to be nothing but thorns and stones, and each one presses upon you and presses into you at the most sensitive places and the farther you carry it the worse it gets. ' A man that studieth revenge,' says Bacon, the great philosopher, ' poisons his own wounds which otherwise would heal and do well.' Suppose Mrs. Grump did say that your new hat was a fright and made you look plainer than ever ; suppose that after all your years of service to the church you were passed over for some upstart who only came yesterday ; suppose that John did forget to see how nice the dress looked of which you were so proud, will brooding and fretting make things any better ? It is a very good thing to forget it.

Getting Your Own Back

Have you not found that true ? Someone did you a bad turn and you kept on thinking about it, planning to get your own back. What happened ? It grew and grew until what was at first a small and trivial thing became a mountain of shame and trouble. It was only a scratch, as Bacon says, it would have healed and done well, but the poison of bitterness and hate was rubbed into it and inflamed it until your whole life was poisoned and you were sick from head to foot with it.

The people who did you the injury were no worse for the way you took it. That was the amazing part of it. You were not getting your own back on them but on yourself. They did not lose any sleep over it. You were the person who lay awake tossing and thinking, thinking and tossing and got up more tired than when you went to bed. You refused to be friends with them. Well, they never valued your friendship so they did not feel it was any great loss. You would not speak, but they did not want you to speak ; you would not look at them, they were glad if you did not. You would have no more to do with them, and the only result was that they were made more comfortable. That is what we call getting our own back. What a blessing it is to have a bad memory for slights and insults.

If you bear a grudge against those who have hurt you what satisfaction they get out of it. ' I touched her on the raw,' they chortle, ' I made her sit up. I put her in her place and let her know I am as good as she is.' They feel very proud and imagine they have done something very fine. That kind of person always does. Why please her by letting her know she hurt you ? Nothing is as annoying as trying to annoy someone who refuses to be annoyed ; trying to offend someone who will not take offence.

No Proper Pride

But if I act like that, you protest, people will think I have no proper pride and will put upon me. Let them think what they please. The thing that matters is that you cannot allow someone else to spoil your life, whatever they may think of you. If the ' Bisto Kids ' with their soap-box look very sniffy and superior at the fur-clad people in the ' Rolls-Royce,' as they surely will, it all depends on how the people in the motor car take it. If they enter into the spirit of the joke and laugh at it they enjoy it as much as the kids do and the children feel that the insult has been a joke and not an insult. But if the ' Rolls-Royce ' people look as superior and important as their car it is not they who really triumph, it is the children. It is as true of proper pride as of all other worthwhile things ; you only save it by losing it ! When Abraham Lincoln was President of the United States it was reported to him that a popular politician had said that the President was a very ugly man. Most people would have been very touchy on the question of looks if they had had Lincoln's collection of features, but he brushed it aside with a wave of his hand, ' Did he ? Perhaps he was right ! ' Life is too short for us to worry over things like that, and we all need to pray for the blessing of a bad memory, or, if you will, a good forgetory. And for all the hurts and slights of life there is one sovereign remedy, and you all know it—

> Do thy friends despise, forsake thee ?
>   Take it to the Lord in prayer,
> In His arms He'll take and shield thee,
>   Thou shalt find a solace there.

XXVII

PRISON CHOIRS

I READ in my paper the other day that a musical service, I think it was a Carol service, had been broadcast to a prison and that hymn-sheets were supplied to the prisoners and they joined in the singing with great heartiness and enthusiasm. I am sure they did. It set me thinking of many things.

I remember among other things, all the great books which have been written in prison. John Bunyan's *Pilgrim's Progress* heads the list, of course. It was written while he was a prisoner in Bedford Gaol and had its origin in a sermon he preached to his fellow-prisoners. And the magistrates had sent John Bunyan to prison to stop him preaching. ' He that sitteth in the heavens shall laugh ' (Psalm ii. 4). Did not John write the book of the Revelation from the prison on the isle that is called Patmos, and Paul write some of his greatest letters from his prison in Rome ? ' Stone walls do not a prison make.' And one could go on to tell of Dr. George Matheson, who, from the prison of blindness wrote, ' O love that wilt not let me go.'

Fanny Crosby (Mrs. F. J. Van Alstyne), who was blind from a baby through a doctor's blunder, wrote nearly 2,000 hymns, including, ' Behold Me standing at the door,' ' Pass me not, O Gentle Saviour,' ' Rescue the perishing.' What a commentary that is on songs in the night ! If you ever feel that you are imprisoned within four walls with not much chance and no prospects, in a prison of narrow circumstances, read about Paul and Silas in prison at Philippi. (Acts xv.) Some of the greatest books and some of the sweetest songs have come out of prison. ' God never closes a door but He opens a window,' says an old Spanish proverb.

At Midnight

And I notice this ; that Paul and Silas sang at midnight. Here is an added wonder, not only prison songs but midnight music. What do you make of that ? Their backs were all torn and bruised from the flogging ; their feet were fast in the stocks so that they could neither stand, nor lie, nor sit in comfort ; it was midnight when all the tides of life run low—and they sang praises to God. We would give a deal to know what they sang. It must have been one of the old Jewish psalms ; it was the only hymn-book they had, Hymns Ancient and Modern, the Crusader's Hymnal, Sankey's and the Methodist Hymn-Book all in one. But they probably sang, ' God is our refuge and strength ' (Psalm xlvi). Maybe, when they had warmed up to it, they even sang, ' O give thanks unto the Lord, for He is good, for His mercy endureth for ever ' (Psalm cvii).

Believe it or not, there are people like that. Robert Louis Stevenson was always ill, often too weak to speak, always fighting on what he used to call, ' the Battlefield of the Bed and the Physic Bottle,' praying that he might be forgiven,

> If I have faltered more or less,
> In my great task of happiness.

' This is our post,' he said of his prison, ' and our

business is to make happiness for others.' What is our faith worth unless ' at midnight,' ' Faith lends its realizing light.' ' There's nothing like a happy song to cheer the way,' the children sing in Sunday School, and they are right.

The Prisoners Heard

' How shall we sing the Lord's song in a strange land ? ' the Jewish exiles lamented. (Psalm cxxxvii. 4.) ' But,' Dr. Rendel Harris comments, ' who knows what would have happened if they had tried ? ' One thing we know, if they had tried to sing the Lord's song, that Psalm would have had a different ending. Paul and Silas did it, ' and the prisoners were listening.' (R.V.) Your yard, your housing estate, your factory or mill, may be as strange a land in which to sing the Lord's song as Babylon was to the Jews. But try singing and see what will happen. There will surely be somebody listening.

Do you remember what a terrible time Christian had going through the Valley of the Shadow of Death until he heard someone singing somewhere ahead of him in the valley ? Then Christian cheered up, ' Because,' says Bunyan, ' he gathered from thence, that some who feared God were in this valley as well as himself. Secondly, for that he perceived God was with them, though in that dark and dismal state. And why not, thought he, with me ? though by reason of the impediment that attends this place, I cannot perceive it. Thirdly, for that he hoped (could he overtake them) to have company by and by. So he went on and called to him that was before ; but he knew not what to answer, for that he also thought himself to be alone. And by and by the day broke ; then said Christian, " He

hath turned the shadow of death into the morning." '
Sing a song of the goodness of God in the four walls of
your kitchen, sing at midnight, and other prisoners will
hear, and who knows what will happen ? There was
an earthquake at Philippi and prison doors were opened
and the gaoler was converted !

XXVIII

DISCONTENTED PEOPLE

' LORD,' confessed a wise old saint, ' I often thought I
did well to be discontented, but I have found that
usually I was discontented with the wrong people and
the wrong things.' How much better the world would
be if only a few more people would learn that lesson.
There is so much to be said in praise of discontent, as
long as it is properly guided. There are always plenty
of people ready to say, ' Things are as they are, and
they can never be different,' and never enough
people saying, ' Things need not be as they are, and
they may be different.'

When children worked twelve hours a day in the
mills and went to work at seven years of age the
problem was the people who were contented ; reform
came through the discontented people. The real hind-
rance in the fight against sin and the devil are the
people who say ' You can't change human nature. You
can't make a silk purse out of a sow's ear.' But
suppose it is not a sow's ear after all, but only a piece
of silk which has been trodden in the mud, what then ?
The condemnation of Dives is that he was content

that Lazarus should be neglected. Discontent makes
people want to do things.   Everybody in Jerusalem
agreed that the state of the Temple courts was an abomination and that the administration was a scandal.
' But what can we do ? ' they said.   Jesus took a
whip of small cords and cleansed it. The woman who is
too easily content is not the best wife and mother in
the street.   Look at her curtains, her doorstep, her
children.   We used to be taught to pray that we
should be content with the state to which God has
called us. Are you sure ?

Discontented with the Wrong People

It is so easy to be discontented with other people,
especially the people next door. Look at them and
the way they live ! We could live their lives so much
better than they do, spend their money so much
more wisely, bring up their children so much more
respectably, treat their husbands so much more sensibly.
It is no wonder the poor man is so bad-tempered and
spends so much time at the Blue Lion.   We are all
clever at living other people's lives. But have we made
such a conspicuous success of our own.   Mr. Micawber
was quite capable of teaching the Chancellor of the
Exchequer how to conduct national finances, but he
could not manage his own pocket money.

Suppose that we grew more critical of our own lives
and our own affairs. Somehow, it never occurs to us
that we might change our ways or that any one is
justified in expecting us to be different. Even if we
do fail in patience and thoughtfulness, in kindness and
love, there is abundant excuse for us. We do not
criticize ourselves, we are so delightfully contented with
our own lives and the way we live them. Do you

remember the story Jesus told of the Pharisee and the publican ? (Luke xviii. 9-14.) The only thing wrong with the Pharisee was that he was discontented with the wrong people. ' Lord gi'e us a guid conceit of ourselves,' the Scotchman is said to have prayed. It is wiser to pray, ' Lord, make me discontented with myself, for until I am discontented I shall never strive to be better.'

Discontented with the Wrong Things

We get discontented with things without instead of things within. We get discontented with clothes and wall-paper ; especially clothes. There is nothing wrong in that. I shall never loose my admiration for the colliers' wives in the Rhondda who papered their kitchens twice every year in the struggle to keep clean or the love that people in the Black Country have for gaily coloured papers because there is so little beauty in their surroundings, and it is every woman's duty to dress as well and becomingly as she can ; and the modern shop window is often an inspiration to praise.

The peril is that we make this a substitute for being contented with the wrong things. It is so much easier to change the wall-paper than it is to change the spirit of the home. It is so much easier to wear a pretty frock than it is to cultivate an attractive character. It is so much easier to try to make a good impression with the clothes we wear than it is to make a good impression by the way we treat other people, especially those with whom we do not agree. It is so much easier to want a new organ than to want new members ; to work for a renovation scheme than to work for a revival.

Discontent is divine as long as we are discontented with the right people, as long as it begins at home.

Then we find that we are so busy putting ourselves right that we have little time to spare in which to grumble about other people. It is splendid as long as we are discontented about the right things; the inward instead of the outward. If we put the inward things right the outward will take care of themselves. Make the tree good and the fruit will be good. (Matt. xii. 33.)

XXIX

IF ALL GOOD PEOPLE WERE PLEASANT

DR. W. L. WATKINSON used to tell a story of an advertisement which ran, 'Domestic Servant wanted: Christian, cheerful, if possible,' and you felt that whoever inserted that advertisement wrote it with a feeling that the quest was hopeless; that Christianity and cheerfulness never could dwell together in the same personality. Numbers of people seem to feel that goodness and glumness are the same thing, and that any godly man or woman must of necessity be serious and solemn, especially solemn. One has boundless sympathy with the small child who is said to have prayed: 'Lord, make all the nice people good, and all the good people nice.'

Attractive Goodness

Have we forgotten the Lord Jesus began His mighty works and manifested His glory by turning water into wine that a girl's wedding breakfast might not be spoiled? Was that not being pleasant as well as good, and in it did He not set us an example that we might follow His steps ? If her goodness does not make a woman thoughtful, tactful, kind, and courteous, her religion is like the ' something just as good,' which the grocer tries to sell you when he is out of stock of the real thing. It is a substitute and a caricature and spoils instead of helping things.

The Apostle John's impatient outburst was abundantly justified. ' He that loveth not his brother whom he hath seen, cannot love God whom he hath not seen.' The only real test of our faith is that we love, that we are good to live with. If people are as prickly as thistles and as uncomfortable as a bed of nettles, there is either something wrong with them or with their religion and you may be sure that the fault is not with their religion. That is especially true of our own folk. We dress up when company is coming, or when we are going out. But when there is no one to see us but our own people we feel that they do not matter. Of course, we should not like Mrs. Somebody from Suburbia to see us in that state for worlds, but it is only pride. So with minds and tempers ; if we have a worse side, an ugly, prickly, unpleasant side, we are very careful to hide it from the world. But it is another thing at home. That is why there are no quarrels like family quarrels, unless they are church quarrels. If only we would learn that one great purpose of our faith is to make us pleasant, easy to live with, to teach other people to smile and to make them feel that the world is not too bad a place, and that life is worth living after all. ' If all the good people were pleasant.'

The Rewards of Pleasantness

If you live in that way it is wonderful how much you get out of life and how abundantly the pleasantness comes back to you. Life grows pleasant when you have learned how to be pleasant. In a very real sense, we carry our own atmosphere about with us and make our own wealth. 'The man who is wrapped up in himself makes a very small parcel,' says a modern proverb, and, one may add, he is usually a bundle of misery. Even if being pleasant is not easy it is splendidly worth while. ' Blessed are they who smile when they feel like frowning, for they shall be called God's heroes.'

A smiling face and a pleasant disposition is one of the finest commendations of religion ever preached. We forgive a woman a score of faults if only she has charm, pleasantness, attractiveness. And what is charm but translating into daily life, ' By love serve one another.' The woman who has charm is she who has goodness enough to be pleasant. She gives you a little bit of flattery and consideration. She treats you as though you were somebody important ; someone who really matters. She puts herself at your disposal and listens to your troubles. She inquires about your rheumatism, and listens sympathetically to the story of your troubles with your landlord, and comments on your new hat. In a word, she makes herself pleasant.

Is not that where so many good people fail ? They cannot be bothered to be patient with your small matters, or to take an interest in your affairs. They try to give you the impression that they are concerned with other matters of far greater importance. But can they claim that they have the mind of Christ ? His was not the goodness which removed Him far from the common things of daily life. So often good people feel that their goodness gives them a privilege, if not a responsibility, of speaking their mind, as they call it. But the mind which they deliver is not pleasant and someone else's soul is bruised. The ill-timed truth we might have kept, who knows how sharp it pierced and stung ? Yet if, through fellowship with our Lord, we have His mind and His Spirit, we shall surely capture something of His Spirit of pleasantness which made it impossible for Him to be hid. We shall be of the fellowship of those of whom it is written : ' She was naturally kind, but she took trouble to be more kindly still.' When we learn not just to do good things but do good things pleasantly, we multiply both the value of our service and our own happiness, for those whom we treat pleasantly treat us pleasantly also.

> If all the good people were pleasant,
>   And all pleasant people were good,
> The world would be nicer than ever,
>   We thought that it possibly could.
>
> But somehow 'tis seldom or never,
>   The two hit it off as they should ;
> The good are so harsh to the clever,
>   The clever so rude to the good.
>
> So friends, let it be our endeavour,
>   To make each by each understood,
> For few can be good like the clever,
>   Or clever, as well as the good.